CW01648466

always next year no4

always next year no4

The 2001-02 season
according to *When Saturday Comes*

WSC
When Saturday Comes
BOOKS

First published in 2002 by WSC Books Ltd
17a Perseverance Works, 38 Kingsland Road, London E2 8DD
www.wsc.co.uk info@wsc.co.uk

ISBN 0 9540134 4 1

Printed by Biddles Ltd, Guildford, UK

Edited by Andy Lyons and Mike Ticher
Cover by Tim Bradford
Design by Doug Cheeseman
Thanks to Tom Davies, Shane Simpson and Richard Guy

contents

Arsenal	The Loneliness of the Long-Distance Gunner *David Stubbs*	11
Ireland	Points Failure *Brian de Salvo*	21
Walsall	All Abroad *Paul Giess*	29
Ukraine	Digging for Victory *Dan Brennan*	37
Rangers	Symbol Minds *Alex Anderson*	47
DC United	Fast Forward *Ian Plenderleith*	57
Press box	Too Close for Comfort *Mike Ticher*	63
Man City	Converts' All-Stars *Ian Farrell*	75
Standard Liège	Taking the Michel *John Chapman*	85
Luton	Surplus Valois *Neil Rose*	93
St Pauli	Of Arses and Buckets *Matt Nation*	101
Reading	Royals Flush *Carolyne Culver*	111
Raith	Lost and Found *David Wangerin*	121
Falkirk	Bairn Necessities *Paul Hutton*	131
Czech Republic	Dry Run to the Top *Kevin Fenton*	141
Holland	Bitter Orange *Derek Brookman*	151
Bilston	Queen Street Blues *Steve Field*	157
Retiring	Down and Out *Neil Wills*	165

introduction

If you finish this book in an optimistic frame of mind, that may be because it includes an unusually high percentage of contributions about clubs that won things last season. Apart from Arsenal, the somewhat haphazard nature of the selection process also threw up a club in each division of the English league who would go on to win promotion.

Against that are ranged rather fewer miseries: a Scottish First Division relegation struggle (though even that turned up some unexpected silver linings), harsh times for a people's favourite in the Bundesliga and a worrying threat to the existence of a midlands non-League club.

But whatever the experiences of fans of individual clubs, it could hardly be said that the 2001-02 season left anyone with a very warm glow. The collapse of ITV Digital will surely come to be seen as the event that most clearly symbolised the end of the long boom that began in the early Nineties. The start of that boom demonstrated a previously unimagined appetite for televised football among British viewers; the end of it showed equally clearly that that appetite had limits. It was shocking news for Carlton and Granada, but how could they have possibly known that games such as Rotherham v Gillingham would not draw a bumper audience?

The end of the era that saw ever-increasing fees for TV rights is not necessarily a bad thing, despite the immediate crisis it caused among some Football League clubs. If it means some of the hype and bombast surrounding the selling of football cools, then so much the better. Similarly, it may mean clubs having to rethink their attitudes on a whole range of issues to do with player recruitment.

It is obvious from this year's contributions that the worldwide movement of footballers has become ever more fluid and has reached ever more incongruous levels. Raith Rovers rely on a charismatic Spaniard up front; Walsall experiment with Brazilians, Portuguese, Australians and diverse others, while missing out on the local talent; the new Ukraine champions Shakhtar Donetsk have a Nigerian leading their attack; Luton's most striking player of the season is a Frenchman, while there is uproar in Ireland over the registration of a Ugandan international with St Patrick's Athletic; an American and another Frenchman are at the centre of racial and sectarian conflicts between Rangers and Celtic fans in Glasgow. And so on.

With so many different permutations, with wildly varying degrees of success, it is hard to say that this freedom of movement is unreservedly a good thing. In some cases, such as Walsall's, it seems to have been taken beyond the realms of common sense. In others, such as the Old Firm, it appears to make little or no difference to entrenched views. But while it is hardly a major contribution to world peace, Kevin Keegan's successful pairing of Eyal Berkovic and Ali Benarbia at Manchester City shows that in its increasingly bewildering diversity, football can at least rise above political conflict, even if it cannot do much to defuse it.

As usual, there is not much in this book about the Champions League or the goings-on at the clubs which occupy so much of the attention of the media in the UK. If *Always Next Year* has a point (no correspondence will be entered into on this issue) it is simply to show that however bloated and feverish the game becomes at the very top, it is always sustained by connections that are local, personal and traditional. Can those unfashionable ways of following clubs survive in an increasingly global, commercial and short-term football world? Yes, when it is simply a case of adopting a frustrating French talent as one of Bedfordshire's own. No, when the pressures are such that small clubs, whether in Scotland or the west midlands, simply cease to exist.

The fall-out from the current financial crises might mean football is taken down a peg or two, which can only be a good thing. On the other hand, it might mean there are more towns where there is no longer a senior club at all. Maybe next year will tell.

Andy Lyons and Mike Ticher

the loneliness of the long-distance gunner

david stubbs

Being an armchair Arsenal fan in a Double year can be as stressful and disconcerting a fan's experience as any. No, really

Ah, the Double. At long last, the parched cries of "How long?" from the wilderness of runner-updom to a seemingly indifferent deity had been answered. Four long years of hurt, never stopped me dreaming.

I hoped it would be so different from last time. I cast my mind back across the misty expanses of time to 1998, a bygone era when Ferguson, Wenger, Beckham and Owen ruled the footballing roost, when pop music was dominated by dispensable boy and girl bands and young people were consumed by mobile phones, Playstation and the internet. The referee had just blown for full-time in the Cup final against Newcastle, a game in which it was only with two minutes of injury time to go, with Arsenal defending a slender 2-0 lead, that I finally believed they would very probably win and the knot in my gut loosened a little.

I let out a leery cheer/jeer (of the sort that makes fans of successful teams so universally popular), for although I was among friends, I wasn't among friends – I was at the shared flat of Leeds and Brighton fans, who had viewed the final with surly indifference, muttering unwarranted imprecations about the validity of Anelka's decisive goal, and weren't in any mood to share my glee. I took what little relish I could in their misery at not having been afforded the opportunity to roast me unmercifully. Then, as they switched channels and subjects, never to dwell one further second on that football match in their lives, I was left alone to bask in the reflected glory of Arsène Wenger & Co's triumph. Wandering out alone on to a balcony overlooking the rooftops of Chalk Farm, I took in a deep, mildly polluted breath of the balmy north London air.

We'd done it. Ah, yes.

Woooooh!!

Woooh!

Wooh.

Woo . . .

Four intakes of breath and the moment was gone. All that Heaven allows. Four draughts of self-satisfaction in exchange for six months of nervous tension, before my inner demons began to rear up and sneer at me. In ancient Rome, when a general returned triumphant from battle to receive the cheers of the populace, it was customary at the victory parade for a slave to be at his side, whispering to him reminders of his mortality and relatively humble status in the vast scheme of things, in case he got too big-headed. Such were the voices that assailed me. "Graham Greene wrote that success is merely delayed failure," said one. Another reminded me of the poet Oliver Goldsmith: "The paths of glory lead but to the grave." A third put my part in Arsenal's Double-winning achievement into unwelcome perspective. "I don't know what you're feeling so smug about, it had nothing to do with you, you silly little sod."

It was true. Down on the street below, a 12-year-old boy in an Overmars shirt cycled jubilantly by. I thought about waving to him but, wreathed in melancholy, didn't have the heart. I rejoined my friends in the living room and tried to drown my sorrows in cheap Cava.

There's a particular sort of pain that comes with being a particular sort of fan. One that doesn't get along to games very often, in fact hardly at all and yet, when watching (or often as not listening to) games is reduced to a white-knuckled, nervous coughing blather of demented partisan frenzy – more so, indeed, than the so-called hardcore fans the camera scans at games, who often seem strangely cheery. Why?

My name is David and I am an Arsenal fan. Glory-seeking this ain't. I never asked them to be successful. I began supporting them in the 1974-75 season, when still casting around for a club with whom to throw in my lot. I disowned Leeds as, although I was brought up there, I was born in London and considered myself an exile from the capital. My father told me that Pete Murray supported Arsenal and, deeply impressed at that DJ's swinging hipster credentials, switched to the Gunners in the hope that some of Murray's coolness might rub off on me. From such acorns of fatuity mighty allegiances grow. Back in 1975, Arsenal finished 16th in the First Division and their mainstay was Trevor Ross ("a tiger in midfield" according to *Shoot*). I stuck with them, nonetheless, through thick and thin (even weathering a moment of Eighties disillusionment when Pete Murray, my Gooner mentor, declared on TV "May God have mercy on your soul if you vote Labour") and, in recent years, through thick and thick. Which has only intensified the agony and expectation.

For many years, I never went to games for the reasons many football fans don't – geographical distance, lack of funds, a brief period of relative indifference (I was in Barcelona the weekend Arsenal played Liverpool in 1989, during which I'd not once wondered how the chaps had got on). In more recent times, with the rise of the Premiership and Arsenal within it, getting tickets to Highbury would seem to be a virtual impossibility for those who haven't been season ticket holders since about 1985. And so, unable to afford the time or effort, I've been reduced to armchair status.

Now, "armchair" implies a cosy state of affairs, yet in practice is anything but. The valiant supporter of the smaller team may complain about the privations of trudging to shed-like stadiums when the rain is coming down like stair-rods, to watch their team play like they're wearing wellington boots, perpetually stuck in the mid-table mud from season to season. However, there are numerous benefits: the camaraderie; the cheerily low level of expectation; the rueful sense of irony. There's also the sense that, whether bellowing at a dozy No 11 who's gone all glassy-eyed when he should be making darting runs infield, or deriving a certain self-righteous pride that comes from involvement in campaigns to sack/back the manager or the board, or prevent ground relocation, you can feel you've made a difference.

None of this for the armchair Arsenal fan. No pride, no self-righteousness. It's the worst of all worlds – no sense of involvement when things go well, no sense of being able to influence events when they go wrong. What you do have is the burning, stigmatic shame of being a Gooner, that most derided and ignoble of creatures. Other Premiership teams don't have it so bad. For often spurious and outmoded reasons, they have their romantic aura that draws affection even from neutrals. Newcastle – howay, good old Bobby Robson. Liverpool – fans worth a goal a game, never walk alone. Chelsea and Spurs are seen to exude a spivvy, stylish Cockney panache.

Lacking any such extra-footballing component (not even the prawn sandwich glamour of Man Utd), and despite the metamorphosis that has occurred under Wenger, Arsenal command no such affection. We're seen as a tight, hostile, joyless brigade who play the game in our tight, hostile little stadium as if motivated by no other desire than to win. Arsenal supporters are regarded as churlish, misshapen, overweight, bald potatoheads, like an army of botched Nick Hornby clones. We are the bad guys.

No one likes us. I do care. Not least because there is some truth in the accusation. Arsenal are unromantic. Despite Bergkamp's balletic wonder goals, despite Vieira's loping elegance, we still seem like a "small", unaristocratic team who have got too big for our boots. Moreover, it so happens that my description of the average Arsenal fan is pretty much an identikit profile of myself. I would be very much at home at Highbury. Among my people. Which is perhaps one of the reasons I stay away from the place, why none of my mates are Arsenal fans. I cannot confront what I truly am. A bastard Gooner.

And so, come August 2001, I found myself facing another campaign, alone and friendless in my Arsenal fixation, racked by self-loathing, joylessly addicted to their continued success. There are times when I yearn for the days of the mid-Nineties, when a place in the UEFA Cup was an excuse to crack out the champers. That, sadly, will no longer do. What once seemed like unimaginable luxury has now become staple necessity. Mere second place in the Premiership and automatic Champions League qualification is not enough. Moroever, the stench of the joyous mockery that was heaped on me that night in front of the big screen in 1999, when Bergkamp fluffed that penalty and Giggs, damn his hairy chest to Hades, went on that once-in-a-lifetime run through the Arsenal defence, still lingers. The ringing cheers of neutrals who hated Arsenal even more than they did Man Utd still echo.

Most of my vivid memories of 2001-02 are of defeat. I recall sitting alone in a bathtub, the water going tepid around me that December night as Radio 5 Live bore the ghastly tidings of Newcastle's turnaround at Highbury, culminating in Laurent Robert's breakaway goal to make it 3-1. The sense of being unable to control these terrible events was palpable. That I should have chosen that moment to take a bath, naked, shivering and vulnerable, in Arsenal's hour of need... Worse, however, was Charlton's 4-2 Sunday defeat of the Arse. I'd left them apparently well in charge of that one and nipped into town. As I sat in the back of a black cab the driver, quite gratuitously, a smile playing about his lips, asked if I wanted to know the current score of the Arsenal v Charlton game. (How did he know I was a Gooner? Do we exude a scent?) Uneasily, I said, "Go on, mate." "Four-one." "You're taking the piss," I said, but something in my voice betrayed that I knew this was not so. His account of events was all too plausible. I couldn't bear to ask him to switch on the radio. And so there I sat in a Fleet Street traffic jam, sealed in an upholstered tomb of despair.

Doubly galling was the sense of a world laughing the joyful laughter of the just and decent in the face of Arsenal's misfortune. Newcastle's victory was hailed by the neutrals as the possible harbinger of a Premiership triumph for the doughty, loveable Magpies. Cheery Charlton's victory, meanwhile, was mud in the eye from all those plucky little two-bob Premiership teams fed up of having sand kicked in their faces by the "elite". I felt like Dick Dastardly as Penelope Pitstop sails past him to victory in *Wacky Races*, both times. Drat! And double drat.

The Dastardly effect was redoubled the night Juventus's reserve team played Arsenal in the match that sealed our European fate. As the Arse played like lethargic, dejected men already aware of their demise, the incessant barking of a police dog rang mockingly around the stadium, a sort of canine cacchination, a snickering commentary on Arsenal's capitulation. It was as if Muttley were in the employ of the Turin *polizia*.

The first defeat to Deportivo La Coruña, 2-0 away, provoked a different sensation in my bosom – cold contempt, an almost consoling sense of disenchantment. It seemed as if Arsenal had almost willed their defeat, that they were happy with their place in the script as perpetual also-rans. It was a moment of armchair epiphany. Clearly, they wanted it less than I did. Why was I getting myself so keyed up for a team with whom I had no geographical or social association; who had visited upon me only derision when they lost and resentment when they won; who often demonstrated as much charm as Mark Thatcher; whom I was, if I admitted it, deep down too ashamed to fully commit myself to (true, it would be tough to get a season ticket for Highbury but had I really tried?); who had egregiously upped sticks from their Woolwich roots a century ago (as a Blackheath dweller, I feel closer to the source of the club than the club itself); a club who neither knew nor cared that I was alive, whose best players were probably only passing through en route to Real Madrid? Why all these decades of hypertension, hyperventilation rewarded with only fleeting moments of elation, just because of fucking Pete Murray?

I deserved better. Briefly, there was a flirtation with Walsall, a dirty weekend at The Valley. I was privileged to see them knock Charlton out of the FA Cup. Such a rare, righteous and refreshing sensation, the triumph of the underdog, unlikely avengers of Arsenal's defeat. Walsall. Ah, yes. A footballing experience of integrity, decency and wholesomeness. It would be like disowning Elton John and initiating myself into Nick Drake. I would attend games – their away fixtures at first – wean myself off the too-rich diet of perpetual Premiership triumph, subsist sensibly instead on the honest turnips of First Division toil. Then I saw them play Crystal Palace, a match of almost hallucination-inducing tedium and decided, sod this. I slunk away without leaving my number.

So, I was stuck with Arsenal. David Seaman. What the hell did he think he looked like? Ray Parlour, face like a knee, curls like a girl, who torpedoed my hopes every time he got possession. Robert Pires, a spindly, poodling milksop who plunged Arsenal into crisis countless times through losing the ball in midfield. Martin Keown, a Cro-Magnon clogger. Sol Campbell, a useless lummox, offloaded on to us by a privately snickering Spurs, a Trojan donkey smuggled into our once fortress-like defence to wreak calamity, whose repertoire consisted of the nervous defensive header and the last-gasp two-footed lunge. The anti-Beckenbauer. Freddie Ljungberg – a blue-arsed apology for a Swedish Goth. Thierry Henry. Shave that wispy 'tache, man, and how did you miss from there? Sylvain Wiltord. Mustard-keen but should be playing for Man City. Patrick Vieira – played half the games like in his mind was already on the plane to Spain. I resented them like brothers.

So I continued my lonely vigil, clutching lukewarm beers in pubs, or, more often, pacing around at home around a radio, begging for whole half-hour chunks of my one and only life to evaporate just so the ref would blow the final whistle. Somehow, over the last few seasons, my sense of self-worth, even mental health, had become intertwined with Arsenal's precarious hold on dominance. Just one slip and they were out there, all of them, waiting to pounce and sneer and mock. Better to endure these things alone – away from mocking eyes and mocking dogs – and in that respect I'm not alone. I have a friend, a Liverpool fan, who also doesn't attend games but won't even watch big Liverpool matches with mates, mumbling by way of explanation that he gets a bit het up and doesn't want his friends to see him in that state. By the sound of it, he's worse than me – I can imagine him, in his living room, stripped near-naked, covered from head to toe in red paint, clutching a stick and bellowing primally at the TV like some fugitive from *Apocalypse Now*, a temporary savage temporarily unfit for civilised company.

Each week brought the fear of failure, offset by relief as Arsenal somehow held on, 2-0, 3-0. An occasional four-goal margin would provide some sort of comfort zone. I hardly noticed, so shell-shocked and gunshy was I from the Charlton experience, that Arsenal were actually putting quite a run together. All a tease, of course. Stop it, just lose, already. Didn't mean that.

Then – another moment of epiphany. A rare opportunity. My brother-in-law, a Villa fan, got me a ticket for their home fixture with

Arsenal. I wasn't sure about going to the away end – it would be an admission of my unfortunate condition. Finally, the choice was made for me – no dirty Gooner, my brother-in-law decreed, was going to infest the Holte End. I was banished to the away stands.

There, however, I found myself among not belligerent potato-heads but a rainbow coalition of decency and diversity. Kids. Genial rastas. Womenfolk. In front of me, a well-spoken chappie of the sort who keeps his cigarettes in a tin. Two seats to the right, a professional-looking young couple in David Clulow specs. Behind me, a geezer with the thickest northern accent I have ever heard, who from his chatter was clearly a lifelong and unselfconscious Gooner. It was like Malcolm X going to Mecca and reconsidering his entire philosophy as his eyes opened to the sheer multi-ethnic range of worshippers.

So much better live – you're so much more in control. And, as Robert Pires scored the greatest goal I've ever had the privilege of being physically close to, chipping the ball over Schmeichel when for one terrible moment it looked as though he'd elected to lob the ball timidly into his arms rather than incur the big Dane's wrath, as the bodies piled down on me from behind and we bellowed dementedly, for one perfect moment I was part of a single, delirious organism.

Nothing much changed, however, during the final run-in – hours of frustration punctuated by seconds of mild relief as goals went in against teams like Bolton, Middlesbrough – and with each final whistle, a pleasure akin to a successful bowel movement. The day Arsenal met Manchester United in what was to be the Premiership decider was full of foreboding. I had already traded defeat in the FA Cup final for the top slot and, thanks to the idiot Ray Parlour and the over-enthusiastic Ljungberg, the deal had been welched on. I mean, it had been nice but...

Come the big day I was more liquid than solid, a pathetic, superstitious fever of mental trade-offs. I forfeited the future option of a first published novel. I threw everything into the grate to try to get a fire of hope going. Then, as the game approached, I felt an unnatural calm, as if in telepathic communion with the Arse organism I had melded with at Villa Park. It will be all right. It will happen. Granted, as I discovered later when watching the TV highlights, United had played their part in the sense of inevitability, playing as if they themselves had been relegated back in March. Taking a tip from Bob Paisley following the 1977 European Cup final, I drank merely tea, savoured the moment.

And this time, it lasted. Not four breaths, not four minutes but 20 whole minutes of sheer Arsenal ambrosia. That's Tantric. What had been at stake? Nothing. What did Arsenal's triumph mean for me? Nothing, except now I'll never have a novel published. What return did I have on all this energy invested? None. What did the Double signify in the broader scheme of things? Sod all. What had I learned from their success? Nothing. Still, the pride bubble only popped when a friend rang and said, "Congratulations." The small boy in me wanted to keep them but the stern father in me demanded I hand them back. What did I deserve? Nothing. Still, for 20 minutes...

Come next season, and it will begin again – anything less than the Treble now will represent a crushing personal disaster and humiliation. Can't wait.

points failure

brian de salvo

This season's League of Ireland champions were... well, it depends who you ask really. But competence in the office certainly counted for more than ability on the field

A gale blows icy rain past my window and wall-to-wall Premiership is on Sky. So why do I decide to drive almost 100 miles to watch two teams I don't support? Welcome to the League of Ireland, where insanity comes with the territory. I'm going to see University College Dublin entertain Cork City. The presence of a university in the Premier Division of the national league adds a certain piquancy to the fixture list, although the College only retained its elite place by winning a relegation/promotion play-off on penalties at the end of the previous season. A bedraggled knot of students at the first leg in Athlone apologised for their lack of numbers with a banner explaining "Everyone else are doing their exams", prompting one lecturer to utter the hope that those so occupied had a better grasp of English grammar.

UCD have had their moments on the pitch. I watched their team of part-timers hold a full-strength Everton side, including Neville

Southall and Peter Reid, 0-0 in the first round, first leg of the European Cup-Winners Cup (pre-match entertainment by the Irish Karate Control Board). But that was in 1984 and at Dublin's Tolka Park, borrowed for the occasion.

The location of UCD's own ground is a closely guarded secret. There is a stadium on campus but it does not host the football club. Instead, their pitch is accessed through a gate bearing the sign "Biochemistry Department", presumably designed to deter those lacking the education to unravel the enigma. Not surprisingly, UCD are the worst supported team in the competition, invariably outnumbered in their tidy grandstand by dedicated away fans bussed into the unknown by coach drivers with privileged information.

The St Patrick's Day encounter with Cork City is advertised in the national press to kick off at 3.15pm. I arrive in good time. But only, it transpires, to see the second half. The start has been brought forward an hour to facilitate the visitors' early return to celebrate the holiday evening in Cork. The rescheduled time has, I am assured, been advertised on local radio. Not on my station it hasn't. Not in the national press either, although that's no surprise; frequent last-minute fixture rescheduling has given published match details a surreal edge. Not so long ago, the sports pages of one morning paper carried a report of a match that was advertised in the same edition as due to be played that evening.

The UCD website also does a good job of keeping punters away from games. The address published in the match programme contains two of those typing errors so beloved of computer intelligence. No way in there. But if you do finally solve the riddle, you can find no fewer than three web pages with matchday information. One informs you that "all matches are played on Thursday evenings at 7.30pm", a second that "all matches kick off 7.45 unless otherwise marked" (none is) and, on the dedicated fixture page, we are told "UCD v Cork City, March 17, kick-off 3.15pm". The Mad Hatter couldn't have done better.

You have to be really determined to watch League of Ireland football. A casual tourist in Galway city centre on the Sunday of the local club's game with Bray Wanderers would have found plenty of posters advertising televised cross-channel matches in its many bars, but not one indicating that live professional football was within walking distance. Fewer than 200 souls with the inside knowledge paid in for that match.

Naturally, none of this marketing mayhem in what is supposed to be part of the Irish entertainment industry makes the headlines here. This season that was not just due to neglect, but also to the fact that there was a genuinely arresting story to be told, namely the Unregistered Players Fiasco. It all began with St Patrick's Athletic and their larger than life supremo Pat Dolan. The ambitious Mr Dolan has done much to raise the profile of domestic Irish soccer, even if rechristening the modestly appointed Pats ground in the working-class Dublin suburb of Inchicore as "The Stadium of Light" does perhaps reveal a tenuous grasp on reality.

We'll stick to the facts. St Patrick's Athletic played their promising midfielder Paul Marney for three games before discovering that he had not been registered. They were duly docked nine points. Cause and effect. Simple? Wrong. Far from admitting this administrative bungle, Dolan responded with a shrill attack, claiming that Marney's form was lost in the post and his club was the victim of a vendetta led by Ollie Byrne, the chief executive of local rivals Shelbourne. Byrne responded that his quest was simply to uphold the "integrity of the rule book".

It was then we discovered that there are no effective rules for the League of Ireland. Its affairs appear to be governed by different sets of contradictory regulations. So the season's progress on the pitch came to be overshadowed by claim and counter-claim, appeal and counter-appeal. Eventually, the league opted to give Pats back the nine points, imposing a fine in lieu.

But that was far from the end of the matter. In fact, the fun was only just beginning. On the morning of Tuesday March 19 Byrne arrived at the League offices with a cheque for €762 (£470) and the authority to scrutinise St Patrick's registration details. This investigation revealed that another player, the Ugandan international Charles Mbabazi Livingstone, had been registered with Pats on September 12. His form carried that date and the signatures of club officials. The only problem was that he had already played five Premier Division matches by then. The Saints were asked to explain this "irregularity".

No scriptwriter could have fashioned Dolan's response. "If clubs are to be deducted points for people who break the rules, then the champions of Ireland would be on zero points and everyone else would be on minus points," he thundered. Uproar ensued. Gerry Cuffe, the secretary of reigning champions Bohemians, reached for the smelling salts and the number of the club's lawyers. The Shamrock Rovers chairman Joe Colwell gave a fair impression of Disgusted of Tunbridge Wells as he recoiled from this "slight on the club's reputation".

Rumours abounded. The former Bohemians manager Roddy Collins, who later escaped to the comparatively sane world of Michael Knighton's Carlisle, mischievously confessed to forging players' signatures in the past and there was a nervous universal shrug in response to allegations that the custom and practice of registration has not always been by the book. But which book would that be anyway? "Once the FAI acknowledges receipt of the registration, liability lies with the FAI," declared Byrne, neatly disowning any administrative responsibility by shifting the onus on to the governing body.

St Patrick's Athletic, meanwhile, appealed to the FAI against the League's inevitable decision to deduct 15 points for the Mbabazi fiasco and furnished the league with a list of 28 other players whose registrations, they alleged, were irregular. Clubs on the Pats blacklist were Bohemians, Shamrock Rovers, Cork City and, surprise,

surprise, Shelbourne. Colwell actually used the "disgusted" word to describe his opinion of Pats. "They are lucky to have been deducted only 15 points – it should have been 24," he insisted.

But wait a moment. If the League of Ireland accepted Livingstone's registration as a St Patrick's Athletic player on September 12, they must have done so in the knowledge that he had already made five unauthorised appearances for the club. Why was nothing done then? Step forward League of Ireland commissioner Roy Dooney with the most sensational revelation yet:

"I found out on September 24 about his late registration and in the light of the negative publicity which surfaced following the Paul Marney problem, I chose to turn a blind eye for the greater good of the league. We had taken a serious PR battering over Marney, the sponsors had viewed the episode poorly and I felt another major scandal was the last thing the league needed. There was a certain amount of risk involved but I felt justified in taking that risk."

Mr Dooney, hired less than a year earlier to give the league a more professional image, comes from the world of politics. So, unsurprisingly, his next statement did not constitute his resignation from a post worth, according to which paper you read, between €75,000 and €85,000 a year. Instead Mr Dooney opted for self-delusion: "I believe I have something to offer the league and I want to carry out the job I was appointed to do. People may feel I made errors of judgement but I felt at all times I was acting in the best interests of the league."

This from a man who was prepared to conspire by concealment in the illegal award of the League of Ireland championship, and the financial rewards that go with it, to a club that had broken the rules of the competition. In many other contexts that would be called corruption. Whatever his sense of integrity, how did he think he would warrant any credibility? But there's more.

The League of Ireland management has opted to introduce summer football with the new season having already begun in July

2002. The reduction of the Premier Division from 12 to ten clubs looks like an attempt by a few solvent members to enhance their financial viability. Six of these ten are situated within 15 miles of Dublin so this protectionist policy, while beneficial to the few, is hardly in the overall interests of the game nationally. The gulf between Premier and First Division standards (and this may sound vaguely familiar) is set to become a chasm.

Clubs cast into the wilderness of the First Division face all the expenses of a national competition on inadequate gate receipts. Consequently the scramble to qualify for promotion this season was a matter of life or death. Two of the clubs involved were Waterford United and Dublin City. Step forward once more, commissioner Dooney, spanner in hand.

Mr Dooney sanctioned Waterford's signing of Shamrock Rovers' Noel Hunt for a second spell on loan, even though the player's initial loan period had expired less than a week earlier. He duly scored a late winner against – guess who? – Dublin City. When the Dublin club protested, the FAI was forced to confirm that Mr Dooney did not know his loan form from his registration document. Waterford lost the three points but Dublin City got no recompense and threatened to resort to law until fear of the potential cost prompted them to withdraw.

So, belatedly, the League of Ireland finds itself seeking to negotiate a deal that will offload Commissioner Dooney. In this era of severance clauses it is no longer possible, it seems, simply to sack a man for incompetence. Eircom, the league's main sponsors, appear to be preparing to bale out.

Pat Dolan was left to reflect that he might have saved everyone a lot of trouble at the outset by enquiring why, if Marney was unregistered on his first appearance, the league had allowed him to clock up two more before notifying his club. Logically (admittedly not a word you would normally associate with the League of Ireland) he might have got away with a three-point deduction and St Patrick's

Athletic would now be the champions. For my money they should be, simply because they were the best team on the pitch and there is no doubt that both Marney and Livingstone are bona fide members of their squad. After the season we've been through, I've given up on niceties like ethics too.

The league stated that there were "no serious irregularities" in the registration of players from other clubs, as Pats alleged. There were tales of one player's name being spelt incorrectly and another's form being misplaced but these were adjudged as "minor errors" not affecting the validity of registration. Just as well, since that way lay madness: the league would end up being won by the club with the most efficient registration secretary.

Despite the fact that the league and the FAI had already ruled against St Patrick's, the process of officialdom still trundled on. An abritrator, Bernard Gogarty, was lined up to rule on whether they should have Livingstone's 15 points reinstated. So we still couldn't be absolutely sure who were the champions of Ireland. The trophy was awarded to Shelbourne although, in a sudden rush of sensitivity, it was thought proper in the circumstances not to congratulate the club on its success. As George Bernard Shaw once said to Holbrook Jackson, author of a racy volume on the contemporary arts scene: "Did all this happen, Holbrook, or did you make it up?"

The sadness is that at the grass roots the game is flourishing in Ireland, with plenty of dramatic and some good football on view, if only you can discover where and when it is being played. Players and coaches are understandably outraged at what has been dumped on them; so much so that Paul Doolin, who combines both functions (and is not to be confused with Pat Dolan) hijacked an acceptance speech to the sporting journalists who had honoured him with an award, to protest publicly at the administrative chaos that disfigured the season.

Doolin's achievement has been to transform a squad of players doomed for relegation at the start of the season into a side of some consequence by the end. His club? UCD. The university team. I'm looking forward to seeing how they get on in the new summer season. If I leave really early I might even see the whole match.

all abroad

paul giess

Walsall's gamble on bringing a taste of Brazil and Portugal to the west midlands proved to be a blunder, but the wrong man ended up carrying the can

For those "small" clubs punching above their weight alongside the Premiership wannabes in the First Division, 2001-02 was a season of distractions on top of the everyday struggle to survive at this level. Matches were played out to a backdrop of the threatened players' strike, persistent rumours of a breakaway Phoenix League and finally the ITV Digital crisis. Industrial action from the players ultimately never happened (although you would never have guessed from watching some of the Walsall squad), while the Phoenix League appears to be on the back burner, if not gone forever, now that we know for sure how few people are interested in watching live football outside the Premiership. And we know this because of the ITV Digital fiasco.

It was a season in which a greater number of clubs than usual seemed to be in trouble even before the TV money dried up. During March an email somehow found its way in to my inbox inviting me to buy a seat at Gigg Lane so that I could forever commemorate the goalless draw between Bury and Walsall in 1993 (a match in which the away fans all stood on the terraces). It was indicative of the general financial crisis that afflicted not just Bury but also clubs such as Swindon and Swansea.

At times like this, the football community draws together to help its brothers in arms. Or do we? At Darlington, the chairman George Reynolds reportedly welcomed the crisis as it offered his team the possibility to move ahead of the 30 to 50 clubs rumoured to be at risk of bankruptcy. There are other frugal chairman who did not rush out and spend money they did not actually have. They probably share Reynolds' viewpoint to some extent, even if they would not admit it in public. In February, Walsall's commercial director Roy Whalley informed the supporters' liaison committee that: "You don't have friends or enemies in football, only interests." What about the supporters of these penny-wise clubs? I pondered this as I debated whether to buy my seat at Gigg Lane.

Since Walsall moved into their new home at Bescot in 1990 we have virtually abandoned the transfer market. The club's record payment is still £175,000 (for Alan Buckley in 1979), even though there have been three promotions to the First Division during the intervening period. Somehow, a succession of shrewd, tactically aware coaches has moulded a never-ending stream of free transfers and triallists into teams that succeeded in taking us from the Third to the First Division.

The 2001-02 season saw us once more attempting to defy the odds and retain a hard-won First Division place. This time we had the biggest fighting fund in the club's history, thanks to the projected millions from ITV Digital. Although it was widely reported that money would be available to build a team, the club's owner Jeff Bonser advocated caution and a reluctance to spend. Instead, Walsall adopted a different strategy, one based almost solely on signing foreign players in preference to developing or (God forbid) buying home-grown talent. It was a strategy that frustrated and alienated the supporters.

Almost as soon as Darren Byfield's play-off winning goal had nestled in the back of the Millennium Stadium netting in May 2001, we began to worry. We had seen it all before, despite the club's promise that "the lessons of last time have been learned". The summer dragged on while we waited for a couple of suitably experienced signings to arrive. Meanwhile, it seems, our director of football Paul Taylor went off on a world tour armed only with the petty cash float. He returned with a bundle of cut-price exotic footballers that – just like a tourist's straw donkeys and sombreros – were revealed to be little more than cheap novelties to be packed away and forgotten within a couple of months.

We suspected it was a flawed policy from the outset, but it was only fair to give the new men a chance to prove themselves. Overseas players have always been capable of generating interest in the lower leagues. Standing on a Third Division terrace and looking at an opposing line-up featuring a Latin American or Mediterranean surname can send a shiver down the spine, even though in all likelihood they would be totally unknown. Sounds exotic – they must be good.

It goes back to childhood when we all wanted to be a Brazilian World Cup star on the school playing fields, adding "inho" to our surnames and attempting ridiculous acrobatic volleys to scuffed, grubhunting crosses. Plenty of people almost broke their backs trying but no one ever scored. But that was just the point. We could not score those sort of goals because we were mere mortals. We were English. Foreigners were special. Brazilians were footballing gods and at Walsall we were more likely to see Martians than Brazilians. This year the management decided to change all that.

When the newcomers arrived they did indeed sound exciting. Their very names conjured up those images of breathtaking solo goals and penalty area acrobatics. Dino Minnelli and Carlos Garrocho just had to be better than plain old Tom Bennett and Jimmy Walker. We even had an actual Brazilian. Trouble was, this was no longer such a novelty. In fact, it was exactly the same policy that we had adopted two seasons previously during our last, failed, attempt to stay in the First Division. In fact, over these two difficult seasons we brought in signings who played their club football on every continent on the planet bar Antarctica. Even Fitzroy Simpson, whom we signed in the week before the kick-off, has opted to play for Jamaica and missed games while on international duty.

The stars of the Primera Liga and Serie A undoubtedly have something to offer our game, but can the same be said of the Portuguese second division or the German amateur clubs that supplied our new signings? Although the names sound exotic, players from the equivalent of our Nationwide League (or below) are no better than what we already have – the proof of this, in our case, being the failure of the new signings to establish themselves in the side.

Adolph Ofodile, the Nigerian striker whose goal had knocked Bayern Munich out of the previous year's German cup, managed just ten league minutes as a sub. Carlos Garrocho started only twice. Both were consigned to the reserves before Bonser revealed at the club's AGM that "Ofodile and Garrocho were both signings with an eye to the future". Garrocho, an Angolan international, is in his late twenties and has been a professional for seven years.

There is another gamble in building a squad so dependent on foreign players – their inevitable "failure to settle" in the west midlands. Ofodile was almost continually plagued with unspecified personal problems. Moreira Herivelto was forced to return to Brazil when his father became ill after Christmas. The Australian winger Dino Minnelli signed in July and left in August when his girlfriend moved over and could not settle in Walsall. You would never have suspected.

Even the foreign players who were already at Bescot seemed to struggle. Last season's top scorer Jorge Leitao lost form dramatically and it was not long before rumours spread around the terrace of late-night exploits in the town centre. The Spanish winger Pedro Matias (surely the only professional footballer whose career path reads: Real Madrid, Macclesfield Town, Walsall) also lost form and failed to hold down a regular place.

By the start of the new year the five new international signings had made fewer than 50 appearances between them and the club was firmly entrenched in a battle for survival for which it was ill equipped. Although none of the new players had commanded a transfer fee, it was clear that most of the club's limited budget had been tied up with their signing-on fees, agents' fees, relocation expenses and the like. Virtually every game was being played with the same squad that was good enough only to finish fourth in the Second Division the previous season. Meanwhile, the promised ITV Digital money would not be touched.

Paradoxically, three of last season's English players – Brett Angell, Darren Wrack and Ian Roper – had been transfer-listed to make way for the newcomers. Fortunately, no clubs came in for them, for they all had to be recalled and went on to play key roles in the side. Roper and Wrack came second and third respectively in the fans' player of the season vote and Roper in particular was sensational in the second half of the season. Wrack scored seven goals and Brett Angell joined in with four, including a 25-yard chipped beauty against Grimsby. Anyone who has watched Brett on his journey around the leagues will find that particular combination of words an unlikely one, but it really did happen.

As the season wore on, unrest became rife across the terraces and mention of anything foreign was met with scepticism bordering on outright hostility. Recognising that something had to change, the club brought in a new midfielder just after Christmas. With news on the grapevine linking us to Paul Evans of the Second Division leaders Brentford, the headline **Saddlers Sign Midfielder** was a joy to behold. After buying the paper, however, joy turned to despair when we discovered it was Carlos Andre, a Portuguese midfielder who had last played in October and had been substituted after 40 minutes in each of his previous two matches. Not the man to throw into an English relegation dogfight in January, one might think. And so it proved, as, despite an encouraging debut in the surprise draw at Norwich, the games seemed to simply pass him by. At least he provided the comedy image of the season by turning out in thick black gloves while wearing a short-sleeved top.

In defence of Andre, there was probably a talented player inside him somewhere, but the mudbaths of an English winter were never likely to be the place to express them. His contract was terminated after fewer than ten games – another poor financial gamble as the points slipped away. What was needed was someone who knew the conditions and was used to the pace of the English game.

In fairness to the club, it is true that even English lower division players are ridiculously overvalued and out of reach for clubs such as Walsall – witness the fees paid for Brett Ormerod and Lomano Tresor Lua-Lua in recent years. However, the midlands does have a competitive non-League scene and gems such as Lee Hughes and Malcolm Christie have been unearthed by clubs willing to look.

The suspicion that Walsall had abandoned this potential resource was highlighted by the success this year of Zat Knight. Premiership-bound Fulham had snapped up the young central defender from our near neighbours Rushall Olympic, just four miles from Bescot Stadium. The transfer fee of a set of new tracksuits was surely within even our modest means. The requirement for the club's general manager Paul Taylor to scout for players only in areas where a high factor suntan lotion is required seemed to have marginalised the suburbs of our own town.

There was no salvation to come from the youngsters among the reserves either. Although there were three or four homegrown players who should have been knocking on the first team door, they were deemed not yet ready for the tension of a relegation struggle.

That may have been because they had not played enough reserve team football, with the second string continually made up of triallists from Sweden, Australia and other far-off destinations. The obsession with foreign players seemed to permeate throughout the club. Finding their path to progression blocked, several of the upcoming youngsters had gone on loan to clubs in the Conference simply to get a game.

It all culminated in one of the saddest days in the history of the club. The sacking of Ray Graydon in January upset not just the majority of Walsall supporters but virtually every other person in football who had come into contact with our honest and respected coach. And coach is the appropriate word to use here. The club's official policy was to employ him to coach the players, who would be provided by Taylor. It was presented as a "European-style" system. However, when it all fell apart, Bonser put the emphasis on "Ray Graydon, the manager" and piled the blame for the club's position on to his uncomplaining shoulders. Taylor, of course, was invited to stay, though eventually he offered his resignation too.

Taylor ultimately left Walsall discreetly in early April. Symbolically, one of his greatest follies, Carlos Andre, left in the same week and the foreign policy now seems to have been discontinued. The new manager, Colin Lee, has brought in overseas players, but only if they already have experience of playing both in England and at First Division level – and, of course, only if they are available on a free transfer.

Although Walsall at no time slipped into an unrecoverable league position, we always seemed to be a good six or more points off anything you could describe as comfort. As the games slipped away it seemed we would be caught out. To survive, we needed to play like champions over the final ten games. So that is exactly what we did, taking 19 points and losing only once. It was no surprise that the half-dozen foreign signings made by Taylor made fewer than five starts between them during this run.

The footballing public of Walsall are not xenophobic. The late-season return to form of previous heroes Matias and Leitao was welcomed with fervour. The occasional gamble on an unproven foreign signing will be appreciated and will arouse genuine curiosity, but we have learnt the folly of building the bulk of a squad around such players.

Fortunately, we did not have to learn it the hard way by suffering relegation. On the contrary, hope for the future has been rekindled and Bonser has been delighted to inform us that the one positive consequence of our cautious transfer policy is that Walsall will not be adversely affected by the ITV Digital problems. He did not go as far as welcoming the problems it would create for other clubs, but as they are "neither our friends nor our enemies" it is surely in our interest if more clubs are forced to behave as we do in the transfer market. We will survive – let's just hope we still have some opponents in seasons to come.

digging for victory

dan brennan

The Ukrainian league is usually boringly one-sided. But a coalminer's son, an Italian maestro and a Nigerian wunderkind changed all that

When Dynamo Kiev fans chanted that there was only one team in Ukraine, there was little that opposing supporters could offer by way of riposte – it was true. Since the collapse of the Soviet Union and the creation of an independent Ukrainian league a decade ago, Dynamo had won nine titles on the trot with tedious predictability. For the last five of those, they had been coached by the doyen of Soviet football, Valery Lobanovsky. Until last year, Lobanovsky had also been coach of the national team, and, as he had done while in charge of the Soviet side, relied almost exclusively on Dynamo players (or ex-Dynamo players in the case of Andrei Shevchenko and Sergei Rebrov) to make up the national side.

The country could be forgiven for thinking it was eternally doomed to watch repeats of the Dynamo Kiev show. However, the 2002 title race finally gave rival fans something to sing about. In a season with more twists and sub-plots than a Dostoyevsky novel,

Dynamo's dynasty started to crumble and another name appeared on the trophy for the first time since 1992.

Local derbies don't mean very much in Ukraine. The only rivalry that really counts is that between east and west. It's born of a mixture of history, culture and economics, more Scotland v England than City v United. Western Ukraine, of which Kiev is part, is mainly Ukrainian-speaking, relatively affluent by local standards and firmly European in outlook. The predominantly Russian-speaking eastern Ukraine, meanwhile, is the country's industrial heartland, fallen on hard times since the collapse of the Soviet Union and still essentially pro-Russian. Such regional antipathies normally make for fierce footballing contests. The main problem in Ukraine was that Dynamo Kiev had been so utterly dominant that no team from east or west has provided strong enough opposition to stir the passions of their fans.

Enter Shakhtar Donetsk. Hailing from the coalmining region of Donbass in the east of the country, they are the ideal counterweight to the aristos of Dynamo. The club's very name, meaning "coal miner", speaks of their industrial roots. Shakhtar have been around in various guises since 1936, but, aside from a solitary cup win, have always seemed destined for the role of best of the also-rans. Their only other claims to fame came from turning out the occasional future star, among them Andrei Kanchelskis and Rebrov; the latter was stolen by Dynamo Kiev as soon as he began to reveal his promise, a fact which still rankles with Shakhtar supporters.

The story of Shakhtar's recent rise is in many ways a remarkable one. But to begin at the beginning we need to go back to May 1995 when Alexander Bragin, a prominent Donetsk businessman and president of Shakhtar, was travelling to watch his team play a league match. Only he never reached the ground, as he was killed by a bomb planted in his vehicle.

The reins at Shakhtar were inherited by Bragin's young protégé, a little-known 30-year-old entrepreneur by the name of Rinat

Akhmetov. Akhmetov was then in the process of carving out a business empire, which over the coming years would make him one of Ukraine's richest and most powerful tycoons and unofficial head of the Donetsk industrial clan.

The son of a local coalminer, Akhmetov is a lifelong Shakhtar supporter. Since assuming control of the club, he has poured countless millions into the club in the pursuit of glory. Eclipsing Dynamo is only the first stage of his vision. His ultimate ambition is to transform the club into a European superpower. While this may sound a tad far-fetched, he has set about achieving his goals with single-minded fervour. Having spent $10 million (£6.5 million) on a state-of-the-art training complex, he is currently planning to build a new 50,000-seat stadium. Shakhtar regularly play to packed houses of 32,000, which, in a country where most premier league teams struggle to pull in more than 5,000, is quite an achievement.

Ukrainian football clubs tend to be run by power elites, but at Shakhtar there is a genuine sense among the fans that they have a stake. Much of the credit for this must go to Akhmetov, who meets regularly with supporters to outline his plans. Despite his status as a rich businessman, he is still essentially seen as one of them.

Akhmetov knew that if his stadium and training ground were to be anything more than huge white elephants, he needed to convert a bunch of promising young players into a team good enough to grace them. He set about his team-building plans in 2000 with a promise to spend more of his millions on some choice foreign signings. A few eyebrows were raised when in December he unveiled Julius Aghahowa, a Nigerian teenager plucked from the relative obscurity of Tunisian champions Espérance for $7 million – a Ukrainian record.

That said, at 17 Aghahowa had already forced his way into the Nigerian national side and caught the eye with three goals in four games in the African Nations Cup, not to mention his extravagant back-flipping. In his first two seasons, Aghahowa defied homesickness and racism to become a firm favourite among the Shakhtar fans. He has since gone on to win admirers further afield, with various English and Italian clubs supposedly queuing up to sign him.

I'd had my first glimpse of Shakhtar the previous season, when they came to Highbury for a Champions League fixture on a bitterly cold November night. As virtual unknowns outside Ukraine, it was a bit of a shock when they swiftly proceeded to go 2-0 up, playing some lightning fast one-touch football that left Arsenal's geriatric defence scratching their heads. Shakhtar eventually lost 3-2 thanks only to an extremely cruel and statistically improbable twist of fate – a late double by Martin Keown. But they went on to show their performance had been no fluke in the return leg, thrashing the Londoners 3-0, albeit too late to take them into the next stage.

The night at Highbury produced a bizarre subplot when Sergei Rebrov, not long arrived at Spurs and doubtless pining for the homeland, turned up at half-time in the away end to cheer on his old team. His attempts at keeping a low profile were unsuccessful; the Shakhtar supporters recognised him at once and he was duly mobbed. Unfortunately, the local police didn't and, assuming he was the ringleader of a band of Ukrainian hooligans, promptly ejected him from the stadium.

While Aghahowa's goals in his debut season were not enough to bring Shakhtar the instant success Akhmetov craved, for the first time they gave Dynamo a real run for their money. As it was, Dynamo's ninth title victory on the hop was shrouded in controversy. With Donetsk topping the table and only a month to run, Dynamo, a point behind, were drawing 0-0 at Metalurg Zaporozhiya. They had not come close to scoring until a shot from the Romanian Florin Cernat hit the post and rolled across the face of the goalmouth. Inexplicably, without even consulting the linesman, the referee awarded a goal. Dynamo went on to win the game 1-0 and the league by one point.

In a country that ranks as one of the most corrupt in the world it is no great surprise that Ukrainian football is tainted by match-fixing and bent referees. It was not the first time that Dynamo had benefited from a dubious decision, but even by Ukrainian standards this one was a shocker. Given that their club president, Grigory Surkis, doubles up as head of the Ukrainian FA, which among other things is responsible for hiring referees, opposing teams were entitled to smell a rat.

Akhmetov was unable to contain his rage: "A championship in which hitting the post can count as a goal as long as it is by Dynamo is not worth very much." He was only voicing publicly what many in the game had long felt to be the case. Surkis maintained – as he continues to do – that his role at Dynamo was purely honorary and that there was no conflict of interest. The actual running of the club, he claims, is handled by the club's vice-president – who just happens to be his younger brother, Igor. It is a sign of just how powerful the Surkis brothers' grip on the Ukrainian football establishment had become, that until Akhmetov came along absolutely no one dared to point out the conflict of interests.

The incident at Metalurg sparked a war of words between the two presidents which was to rumble on throughout the following season. Akhmetov called on Surkis Snr to resign from the UFA. The latter accused the former of sour grapes and of instigating a deliberate campaign to discredit him and Dynamo. Spice was added by the fact that the battle between Donetsk and Kiev is mirrored by a rivalry between the country's two main business clans – in which Akhmetov and the Surkis brothers are key protagonists.

As far as football was concerned, the stage was perfectly set for the following season. With Shakhtar vowing revenge, the duel between the two clubs was being pitched not just as a battle between east and west, but one of Good v Evil, with Akhmetov cast as caped crusader against the empire of the Surkis brothers. For the first time it seemed Ukraine would have a championship capable of capturing the public's imagination, both on and off the field.

Shakhtar started in convincing style, matching Kiev blow-for-blow in the league. At the midway point in the season they remained undefeated and were top of the table, ahead of Dynamo on goal difference. However, they had been in a similar position the previous season, so no one was getting too excited just yet. What's more, they found themselves entering the winter break without a manager. Their league performances could not atone for the fact that they had crashed out of the Champions League qualifying round 5-1 to Borussia Dortmund. To make matters worse, a swift exit from the UEFA Cup followed – 4-2 against the unfancied Bulgarians of CSKA Sofia. Such results did not chime with Akhmetov's plans for European domination. The coach Victor Prokopenko, by his own admission, had run out of steam and ideas, and in September he resigned.

For his next trick, Akhmetov promised to bring in a top European coach, who would be equal in stature to Lobanovsky. While no one doubted the scale of his ambitions, or the size of his wallet, even the most optimistic of Shakhtar fans were sceptical about his ability to lure a fancy dan foreign manager to the Ukrainian hinterland. Jack Walker had managed to bring Kenny Dalglish out of retirement to Ewood Park, but Donetsk makes even Blackburn seem like Paris in the spring. So it was a monumental coup when in January Akhmetov announced that Nevio Scala, architect of Parma's rise to prominence in Italy and former manager of Borussia Dortmund and Besiktas, was to take over as head coach with immediate effect.

Rumours of Scala's appointment had been rumbling on since the previous October, when the Italian had visited Donetsk. It was generally presumed that, after one look at the place, he had booked himself on the next flight back to Rome, never to return. In the meantime, Shakhtar continued to be linked to a long list of high-profile coaches, including the cocaine-snorting Christoph Daum. But after three months of behind-the-scenes negotiations, Akhmetov finally got his man, with Scala signing on for 18 months.

He had apparently turned down a return to Parma and, perhaps less controversially, the chance to take over the Scottish national team. The Italian remained reticent on his reason for choosing a glamour move to Donetsk, except to say that he had found Akhetmov to be "a very nice man" – translated by most people to mean: "He made me an offer I couldn't refuse." In return for a rumoured £6 million sweetener, Akhmetov demanded that his new coach start by winning the double in his first season.

Scala's first act in charge was to dispatch Prokopenko, who had been kicked upstairs as technical advisor, on a scouting mission to South America. Shakhtar fans waited with bated breath during the winter break to see which Brazilian starlet he would return with. However, if luring a top Italian coach to Donbass had been a minor miracle, persuading the next Ronaldo to winter in the Urals was perhaps asking too much and Prokopenko returned with a tan but no new signings.

Not that the fans were too worried – after all, they had Aghahowa and they also had Andrei Vorobei, a lightning fast striker, viewed by most as the natural successor to Shevchenko in the national side. As it turned out, Scala's initial forays into the transfer market were a lot less exotic – a Polish Under-21 goalkeeper and a Romanian-Yugoslav defensive pairing. Glamorous they weren't, but they did bring stability to a defence which had been leaking goals almost as fast as Aghahowa and Vorobei could score them.

In complete contrast to the authoritarian approach of Lobanovsky at Kiev, Scala sought to introduce a relaxed atmosphere among his players. Also in contrast to the Kiev regime, he encouraged openness with the press. One of his first decisions was to hand the captaincy to 22-year-old midfielder Anatoly Timoschuk. The symbolism of the gesture was clear to everyone – Scala was sweeping out the old order.

Perhaps the most intransigent aspect of that old order was the system of scientific post-match analysis traditionally favoured by most Ukrainian clubs. First developed by Lobanovsky in the 1970s, this involved using computer programs and teams of number crunchers to dissect every aspect of each player's performance and generate models for optimum performance. Shakhtar themselves had adopted Lobanovsky's Law with unquestioning enthusiasm, employing no fewer than 11 "scientific specialists". They were soon sent packing in a backroom clearout and Scala brought in an entourage of Italian assistants, fitness coaches and masseurs, promising to instil a "European mentality" into his new charges.

However, in the first months of his reign, the Italian's tactical tinkering looked as though it might cost Shakhtar the title. After his first seven games in charge, Shakhtar remained unbeaten and were conceding fewer goals, but three draws against weaker opposition saw a one-point lead converted into a four-point deficit and the knives were already out. Scala and Akhmetov called for patience. Dynamo were quick to jump on Scala's failure to produce instant returns, with club director Josef Szabo accusing Shakhtar of lacking patriotism by appointing a foreign coach.

In March, Scala had got his first proper taste of refereeing Ukraine-style when Shakhtar had two players inexplicably sent off as they were held to a 0-0 draw at home to lowly Kryvbass. So disgraceful was the performance of the referee – Ihor Ischenko, who happens to come from Kiev – that even Surkis and the Ukrainian Referee's Committee had to agree to a one-month suspension.

For the next two months Shakhtar continued to trail Dynamo in the league, while both teams made it through to the cup final. But before that encounter came yet another twist. On March 13, Lobanovsky, having been rushed to hospital during a league game, died of a brain haemorrhage. A quarter of a million fans turned out to mourn the passing of a legend who had shaped the course of Soviet and Ukrainian football. With no obvious candidate available to replace him, Kiev turned to the former Dynamo favourite Alexei Mikhailichenko, once of Rangers. Popular as he was, Mikhailichenko had no coaching experience – it was surely too much to expect him to fill the boots of a demigod. In the saddest of circumstances, it seemed the balance might finally be shifting to Shakhtar.

Nevertheless, the Donetsk club went into the cup final 13 days later as underdogs. They had lost every one of their away games in the four two-legged rounds en route. Only an inspired hat-trick by Vorobei to clinch a 3-0 home win against Stal, a division and a half below them, secured the 4-3 aggregate victory that prevented an embarrassing first-round exit.

As the cup final is always played in the capital, Kiev had home advantage and Shakhtar were weakened by the loss of Aghahowa and his countryman Isaac Okoronkwo to Nigeria's World Cup squad. But a goal from Vorobei in extra time put Shakhtar 3-2 ahead and, despite having a player sent off half way through the extra period, they clung on for a momentous victory. Scala had worked the first part of his miracle. For Dynamo, who had planned to dedicate their win to the memory of Lobanovsky, it was a huge psychological blow.

The championship was decided by Shakhtar's home game against Dynamo in June. Not surprisingly it was a tense affair, riddled with errors and bookings. And in the end it was errors – two monumental ones by Dynamo – that decided it. Fedorov and Garranchich, normally two of their most reliable players, each contrived to score past their own keeper to give Shakhtar a 2-0 win and send them one point clear at the top. For those in Donetsk and beyond who had yearned to see Dynamo toppled, the manner of their defeat was a sweet moment and it seemed to underline the feeling that these were the last days of a dynasty. Shakhtar finally clinched the title – and with it a historic double – in the last game of the season with a 1-0 win over relegation doomed Zakarpathia.

So confident is Akhmetov that Shakhtar will be regular performers on the European stage that he is building a five-star hotel in Donetsk to house their visitors. "As we are going to be one of Europe's top clubs, we must be able to greet our guests well," he explained to one bemused foreign journalist. "Tell everyone in Europe they are welcome here." Dynamo will be back next season too, of course – but at least now their fans will have to change their song.

symbol minds

alex anderson

The racist hounding of a black Celtic player was only one of the innumerable ways the hatred was stoked in the Old Firm rivalry

I really don't have a lot of time for Dianbobo Balde. As far as I'm concerned, he is to the art of defending what Reggie and Ronnie Kray were to Neighbourhood Watch schemes. When "challenging" an opposition striker for an aerial ball, Bobo tends to use his Jonah Lomu-esque height and physique to power his way through the vertebrae of the unsuspecting centre-forward, arse first. It's just a matter of time until he does some serious damage.

Oh, and he plays for Celtic. And I support Rangers, so there's that whole contractual thing. You know, a whole list of documentary makers, feature writers and social anthropologists – all English – ready to sue the arse off me the moment I fail to fulfil the "most bitter divide in football" stereotype. Express as much as an nth of empathy for the opposite half of the Old Firm and before you can say "It's the way ah wis brought up", your days as a media darling are over.

No more having my head silhouetted by worthy directors. No more having my voice dubbed by a RADA-trained actor. No more Sunday supplement spreads, featuring a picture of me from the neck down, wearing the NTL-sponsored shirt and holding a Stanley knife. No more ready listeners to those tales of my allegiance to the Queen/Pope, my pride in being more British/Irish than Scottish, my admiration of the UVF/IRA and no retelling of my positively Ustinovian anecdote about the day I simply HAD to slash that Japanese tourist. (You know the one. I do it at every dinner party. Remember? The guy accidentally walks into one of our pubs wearing a green/blue strap on his camera and...) After so many years, we Old Firmers just couldn't live without that drug they call celebrity.

So, believe me, no one was more alarmed than I when, on the last day of September 2001, I risked all my Sectarian City credentials by sticking up for Bobo Balde. What was worse, I was at Ibrox at the time. What was unforgivable, it was during the first Old Firm game of the season, and Rangers were losing.

We would lose our first two derbies of the season, thus handing the other horse the SPL title before Christmas. In December, coach Dick Advocaat was "moved upstairs" with more euphemism than purpose and, now under Alex McLeish, we won the third rematch of The Boyne to knock Celtic out of the CIS Cup and ruin their chances of a back-to-back treble. The next two league derbies were drawn and the sixth and final Old Firm match of 2001-02 was the Scottish Cup final, which we won. The on-field Rangers rot has been spectacularly halted, but off-field it continued apace.

The monkey noises, which increased in volume every time Toulouse-born Balde touched the ball on September 30, represented the first of a series of new depths plumbed by the media and opposition fans as well as by the perpetrators in the Ibrox stands. The Rangers supporters responsible for such crass stupidity take sole blame for the abuse itself. I found myself shaking my head more and more vigorously as many of my fellow Bluenoses engaged in an act of overt racism which will never become cliched no matter how unoriginal.

The most pathetic aspect of the whole episode was the fact that Mark Walters had been on the pitch at half-time. Our winger of the late Eighties and early Nineties peformed the up-tempo, showbiz Rangers version of the half-time tombola draw and the red, white and blue punters sang his name and lauded him like the hero he is. When the second half kicked off, Mark was sat comfortably in the directors' box, basking in the warm afterglow of his return. Quite possibly he had the remains of a sentimental tear rolling down his cheek when many of those same Rangers supporters began imitating gorillas and monkeys.

Not only is Mark Walters an Ibrox legend, not only was he the first black player ever to wear the Rangers jersey, not only was he the first black player to grace the Scottish Premier League – he was also the last straw to be clutched by those of us who try to defend Rangers' image. It's crude and patronising in the extreme, I know, but our defensive adoration of a pilloried black player was a tabloid-friendly display of "right-thinking". Such crumbs of mitigation against all that's wrong with the Rangers support have to be ruthlessly seized upon by Bluenoses who care what others think of them.

Before Walters joined the club I had attended games at Ibrox – a midweek friendly against Twente Enschede stands out – where black players were victims of the all-too-familiar tirade of gutteral noises. References to jungles and coconuts were bandied about as if the East Enclosure were at the cutting edge of alternative comedy. But still what made Rangers world-renowned was our hatred of Catholics. Had a black player joined Celtic first, no doubt the positions would have been reversed. But Walters came to Ibrox, and when he played his first game, on January 2, 1988, it was the Celtic fans who had hired gorilla outfits from fancy dress shops and who chucked bananas at him. We secretly delighted as the Celtic support "shamed Scotland" with their small-mindedness.

By the mid-Nineties, however, an all-white Rangers team took on Ajax in the Champions League and Patrick Kluivert – black, brilliant and with a damningly Irish Catholic first name – was given some sickening treatment. It was clear there had not, in fact, been an outbreak of common decency among the Ibrox hardcore. It had simply been a temporary abstention in deference to a black Rangers player who knew how to destroy a Celtic defence single-handedly. By 2001, even that had evaporated. Rod Wallace and Marcus Gayle, squad players by the time of the Balde incident and probably sat in the stand beside Walters, were no deterrent to the sinister abuse.

During the second half of the opening Old Firm game of last season, the sickening taunts and the cries of "black bastard" had become so bad that I turned to the man sat behind me and muttered something like, "You can't do that." In the middle of a Rangers v Celtic game everything is considered justified except sticking up for the opposition in any way. My mumble was taken as an outrageous show of disloyalty, and the only thing I could do to prevent an all-out barney with several blokes (who, like me, were in their season ticket seats and would therefore be sat behind me for the next eight months) was to replace one evil with another: "He's not a black bastard," I said, to my ever-lasting shame. "He's a Fenian bastard."

I won't say this brought about an immediate restoration of friendly relations, but it certainly diluted the chances of me ending up in traction before the end of the match. However, the price I paid for my physical health has shown up as a debit on my moral account. Many of my Catholic friends and relations have often used anti-Protestant jibes in reference to Rangers players, just as I have let slip the odd anti-Catholic version in the heat of an Old Firm battle. I don't hold it against them, they don't hold it against me – we all know it emanates from a unique kind of (anti) social conditioning. But to specify so exactly which type of bigotry I see as acceptable gave me much more existential angst for the rest of the season than Celtic's disappearance over the championship horizon.

The newspapers and TV programmes were concerned with only one "sickening" incident of abuse from that match. Claudio Reyna, the captain of the US national team and a Rangers midfield mainstay before he left to fight relegation with Sunderland, was taking a corner at the Broomloan Road or "Celtic" end of the stadium. Relentlessly replayed TV pictures and front page photographs showed one away supporter, immediately behind Reyna, standing up, with arms outstretched, mimicking an aeroplane – clearly referring to the Twin Towers attacks on New York less than three weeks earlier.

The deluge of outrage duly followed. Websites, radio phone-ins, TV discussion programmes, editorials, columnists and letter-writers all declared their disgust. Some Celtic supporters claimed the man caught on camera suffered from learning difficulties, and others highlighted the fellow fans who could be seen dragging him back down to his seat in shocked embarrassment. Rangers fans suddenly remembered they had in fact seen many hundreds of Celtic fans performing the same sick mime in Reyna's direction and reminded the world how, the previous week, the Celtic support had sung songs asking UEFA to force Rangers to play their UEFA Cup tie against Anzhi Makhachkala in war-torn Dagestan.

On the other hand, plenty of Celtic fans wanted it known how ashamed they were and how sorry they felt for Reyna. Plenty of Rangers fans were willing to say we had the same random idiots within our number and if Celtic had had the only US player on the pitch the same thing would have happened at the other end. But no one wants to hear common sense more than once in this kind of situation – it's boring and it doesn't make newsworthy copy. Instead, we soon saw the Balde-baiting held up as a counter-claim of moral depravity and on went the expressions of horror and disgust from each side. The nasty things that happen in Old Firm games must be exposed to the max, just in case both sides forget how much they're supposed to hate each other. That's the rule.

Come March 2002 and the second Ibrox Old Firm game, the microphones caught an even louder level of monkey chants from the Rangers fans whenever Balde touched the ball. As he approached the Govan Stand to take a throw-in, the cameras caught an even clearer picture of hundreds of red, white and blue-clad morons jumping to their feet and scratching under their arms. It did make the news, but not to anything like the extent that the Reyna incident had. September 11 provided the opportunity for Old Firm hatred to be mixed in with dramatic world events. But now, in March, racism? Against one guy? Nah – did that 14 years ago, thanks.

So the hunt goes on for ever more nauseating ways in which the Old Firm can disgrace themselves and the media can help their respective fans claim the moral high ground. The deaths of Princess Margaret and the Queen Mother came in handy here. On the latter occasion a few Celtic fans at their home match with Livingston provided the audible disrespect required of them, while the self-consciously deafening silence of 50,000 Rangers and Hearts fans the next day provided the perfect counter. There were silences at every other ground in Scotland too, but the actions of Rangers and Celtic supporters are always interpreted as betraying them as republican conspirators or royalist hard-liners. They can't just be idiots.

When Peter Lovenkrands scored an injury-time winner in the last meaningful game of the season, the Old Firm's football for once seemed to take precedence over the Old Firm's fans. However, sitting at Hampden before the Scottish Cup final kicked off, I was witness to an end-to-end contest which was every bit as exciting as the five-goal thriller which followed.

Approximately every third Rangers fan waved a Union Jack and turned half of Hampden into something akin to the Last Night of the Proms. It was a victory for Unionism. But no, across the other half of the stadium the Celtic fans were waving their fair share of Irish tricolours – one back for Republicanism. Then – bang! – the Celts move into the lead by producing the Basque flag: it's got a red background but has some green and white as well and it represents a movement deemed sympathetic to nationalists in Northern Ireland. But, wait a minute, the Rangers fans equalise with the blue and white flag of Israel – an occupying force in a disputed zone that feels itself misrepresented and unfairly vilified by the outside world, a bit like the British Army in Northern Ireland. And, right at the death, some of the Union Jacks flaunted by the Rangers supporters are emblazoned with Golden Jubilee messages and pictures of the Queen.

Nothing is too tenuous to be incorporated into this seemingly endless exchange of sterile symbolism. How can we remedy a situation in which Rangers supporters feel the need to make the reversible England World Cup top the best-selling football strip in Scotland? How can we arrive at a point where I can safely taunt a Celtic fan because we ruined their 100 per cent home record in the last league game at Parkhead without him retorting: "Yeah, but what about the 'gypsy' taunts from your end of the ground every time Moravcik was on the ball?" When will it ever be just about football between Rangers and Celtic?

Well, never, frankly. Partly that's because they are continually meeting in do-or-die circumstances. Why is Liverpool v Man Utd more poisonous than the Merseyside or Manchester derbies? Because they are the two most successful teams in the history of the English game. Was West Brom v Wolves ever as intense as when the two of them fought for the second automatic promotion spot in the First Division? The close footballing rivalry was an aspect of Old Firm history long before the sectarian issue became so apparent. Nowadays, the religious split is simply a ready reckoner method of deciding which one of the two available teams Scottish glory hunters should pick. It comes with free access to a dozen foot-stomping classic tunes which will inspire or disgust listeners with their grotesque lyrics.

The rest of the SPL is sick of us now. If we were to fall into the desperate arms of the Nationwide League, which admittedly now seems highly unlikely, it might prove to be the best thing that could happen to the Old Firm (if not to the First Division). For a start, there would be no guarantee that both would win promotion instantly – if a club with Sunderland's attendances can struggle to stay in the Premiership, I don't see why Rangers and Celtic are certainties to get into it – and that would at least dilute the monotonous cycle of bitterness for a while.

Even in the Premiership there would be only two league meetings a season instead of the current four. And competition from a whole host of clubs who have no century-long culture of fearing the Old Firm, with teams who can give us so many more problems than anyone in Scotland ever could – this would help us see our true place in the world. It would be the most brutal broadening of horizons for Rangers, Celtic and their fans, and it would certainly take the edge off the Old Firm games. We had six "all or nothing" hatefests last season. Such familiarity has bred a contempt which encourages the supporters to continually seek new, more vicious ways of insulting the opposition players and new, more hypocritical ways of demonising the opposition fans.

During the course of 2001-02, Tore Andre Flo had his car vandalised by Celtic fans and the *Daily Record* took great delight in telling the world this was a "revenge attack" after Rangers fans did likewise to Neil Lennon's car. A brilliant piece of gutter journalism this. It managed to express moral outrage while simultaneously inciting Old Firm hatred and managing to give both sets of fans something to feel bitter and sanctimonious about. The phrase "That's just typical of those Fenian/Proddy bastards" could be seen from Edinburgh, rising above the city of Glasgow in a giant thought bubble. Are Rangers and Celtic fans going to stop reading the tabloids? Never. Are they going to start taking the newspapers' wind-ups less seriously? No.

Improbable though it may seem at the moment, for the vitriol of the Old Firm rivalry to dissipate we need to escape Scotland's claustrophobic hate factory and move into the air-conditioned open-plan office of the English league. Until Rangers and Celtic move south of Hadrian's Wall, we will be waiting in vain for the day when the silent majority drowns out the empty vessels at an Old Firm match and when the agent of common sense stands up in the middle of an Old Firm game and says simply: "This isn't right."

fast forward

ian plenderleith

Time flies in the MLS. You have to compress glorious eras and decades of underachievement into a few years, in case it all folds up again

The twin foundations of supporting a football club are tradition and hope. Tradition is represented by the club's past and acts as a bedrock of reassurance to fans that they are involved with an institution that claims its own history and identity, no matter how unglamorous that history is. Hope, on the other hand, is an indispensable accessory even for those moon-faced moaners who stand and watch with their hands deep in their pockets almost praying for defeat in order to fulfil their prophecies of gloom. For even they nurture a smidgen of optimism in their malcontented hearts, otherwise they would not be watching at all.

This makes following a team in the US professional league, Major League Soccer, a difficult proposition for a European fan accustomed to supporting sides that are usually more than a century old and who can, theoretically, move up or down the national league pyramid. MLS began in 1996, so there is little tradition, unless you can remember the failed North American Soccer League of the 1970s and early 1980s, which few can except through reciting a roll-call of ageing but well-paid stars. And at the beginning of 2002, when MLS commissioners met in order to axe two of the 12 clubs (or, more accurately, franchises), the league and its investors committed themselves to continuing the loss-making MLS for only another five years.

Or, put another way, if MLS is still losing money at the end of the 2006 season, its remaining clubs, and thus the league, may well follow Miami and Tampa Bay into extinction. This limits or perhaps eliminates the hope factor, for what is the joy in anticipating your club's future success, even in the short term, if you know that in ten years' time its existence will be just another failed chapter in the struggle to establish professional football in the United States?

Nonetheless, if you are desperate enough to find a club and follow the game here, then you can become involved with an MLS team, as long as you are prepared to narrow your perspective sufficiently. Thus, at the start of the 2001 MLS season, Washington's DC United were "historically" the league's most successful side. In the league's first four seasons they reached the MLS Cup final (you need to pay careful attention here – this is the single game championship-deciding final that follows the play-off knockouts. The play-offs are contested by the top-placed teams from the regular season regional divisions) on all four occasions, winning three times to become champions. In an American context that is a history upon which to build future visions.

But during the previous year, 2000, a curious thing had happened to DC United. Although they boasted approximately the same squad that had taken the championship in 1999, they were thoroughly awful, and failed to make the play-offs. The defence, made up of the bulk of the US national team's back line of Carlos Llamosa, Eddie Pope and Jeff Agoos, leaked laughably, as the team scored a high number of unusual own goals. Bolivian midfielder and club captain Marco Etcheverry, the league's standard-bearer who had led the side to victory from its inception, seemed more interested in complaining about bad referees than creating goals, while midfield workhorse Richie Williams, also a US international, inexplicably looked as though he could barely play at all any more.

No one could explain what had gone wrong, so Llamosa, Agoos and Williams were rashly transferred and everyone talked of a one-off freak season which couldn't possibly happen again. However, the typical calibre of replacement for 2001 was represented by the central defender Mark Watson, a Canadian who had experienced the glory of playing for teams like Oxford United, and the South African Stephen Armstrong, lured to Washington from Watford's reserves.

Having arrived in DC in 1999, just as the side was winning its third championship, it was the lame 2000 season which had endeared United to my loser-liking affections. The scarcity of both goals and victories had made celebrations that much more special. Which is not to say that I did not want them to succeed in 2001. Far from it – success would feel all the more deserved for its comeback nature as the side shed the complacency that had so disabled it the year before.

Yet the 2001 campaign, almost from the start, continued as if the six month close season had never happened. The lacklustre Etcheverry, around whom the side was still built, was typically sent off for a stoppage-time headbutt on Chicago's Dema Kovalenko (who had outplayed and frustrated him for the previous 90 minutes), while the quick but combative US international Ben Olsen was ruled out for the season after breaking his ankle on loan at Nottingham Forest. Re-signed Salvadoran striker Raul Diaz Arce, a success in his first spell at the club, was drafted in as a marketing exercise, but the number of local fans from his native country he enticed back to the Robert F Kennedy Stadium far outweighed the value of his contributions on the pitch. He quickly left for the second time.

Even when DC played well and dominated, as in the return home game against Chicago, they contrived to lose 2-1 thanks to farcical defensive lapses that left the visiting team raising their arms more in disbelief than ecstasy. Occasional flashes of the old DC, such as the 5-0 home defeat of New England and a 3-0 away victory at defending champions Kansas City, were followed by runs of extended mediocrity that saw the side slip away from play-off contention once more .

Yet the league is organised in such a way that, no matter how poorly your side is playing, you never have to give up hope entirely. With no relegation, and with your team only having to finish with the eighth best record of 12 teams to make the play-offs, the mathematical possibility of qualifying, and then going on to become champions, remains an outside reality even when your record reads Played 20, Won 6, Drawn 1, Lost 13, which were DC's stats by mid-August, over two-thirds of the way through the season. Sure, the team was playing crap, coach Thomas "Wrong 'un" Rongen had all the authority and charisma of Al Gore leading an embroidery workshop, and striker Chris Albright, touted as the club's great future hope, had only scored one goal all season. But we could still become champions. We just needed to win seven or eight games on the trot to sneak in.

Pragmatists could tell, however, that this season was over for DC weeks before the two final home games were cancelled following the September 11 terrorist attacks. Fans were reduced to hoping for some kind of glory in the US Open Cup, an 88-year-old, single-tie knockout competition open to both amateur and professional sides. After practice-match disposals of the New Jersey Stallions and the Hershey Wildcats, we half-heartedly cheered a quarter-final win over the A-League Richmond Kickers, and even they pressed us close at 2-1. Then in the semi-final DC finally had to play a fellow-MLS team, New England, and a 2-0 defeat blocked this final, slightly bogus path to achievement.

Still, one more season notched up to the club's past, and now we could boast a history of both winning and losing, like any proper football team. After all, it would have been unhealthy for the fledgling league if DC had continued its dominance of the first four years. And despite the dismal results, we could still dredge up some optimism. Coach Rongen was finally sacked, while United's teenagers Bobby Convey and Santino Quaranta began to show that flair may at last become a word associated with US footballers. The apparently untouchable Etcheverry will be there until he lies down and falls peacefully asleep in the centre circle, and even then it will be a while before anyone notices that his contributions have diminished, but we can always hope that he accumulates enough red cards for a long-term suspension.

As for the league itself, survival will continue to depend on the goodwill of its investors and the efforts of MLS to pull in larger crowds, build devoted football stadiums and to attract and develop decent players despite stringent salary caps. But with that five-year guillotine hanging over us, I'd prefer to channel my expectations more realistically towards challenging for a trophy at least in a half-hearted fashion in the few short years that may be left. In fact, as long as the RFK Stadium continues to offer vinegar with its chips (unheard of elsewhere in the US) and Foggy Bottom Ale as an alternative to Bud Light, then I promise to curb my blasphemous verbals and wait, passive but smiling, for the axe to fall.

too close for comfort

mike ticher

A short spell of covering matches for a national newspaper provoked alarming feelings of empathy for Trevor Francis

At the start of the season I had resolved to get out a bit more. Gripped by a spirit of adventure and needing to see something other than the grubbier bits of London now and again, I offered to get off the sub-editors' bench and do a few match reports for the *Guardian*. Apart from anything else, it was about time I made the effort to do something a bit more like real journalism.

Not that much more, though. I was not about to volunteer for the relatively tough business of a midweek night match, where you have to assemble your thoughts, wrestle with the technology of transmitting reports and render quotes accurately, all against the clock. None of that. This was to be the relatively leisurely task of watching on a Saturday afternoon, mulling over on the train home and filing copy in the morning.

What could be more pleasurable than watching football from a new vantage point and getting paid for writing a few hundred words about it? Well, of course that depends on the game and the surroundings. But the money itself made me slightly anxious. The economics just didn't work. The newspaper was paying me a reasonable sum, plus travel costs, to write a short report on a match, generally from the bottom of the Premiership or the top of the First Division, that could be covered very easily off the wires. Logically, fee plus expenses had to equal the difference in quality between my 500 words and something copied and pasted from the Press Association. How brilliantly witty and insightful were they going to have to be to justify that kind of investment?

September 22
Sheffield Wednesday 2 Manchester City 6
It's 11 days after September 11. And who better than a train full of heavy drinking football fans to tease out the intricacies of the new global politics? Some Fulham fans on their way to Leicester are having an animated discussion about Bin Laden's UK branch. "There's a lot of nutters here too," says one. "The first thing you do, right, is sort things out in your own country." By the time we file out of Sheffield station someone else has developed this theory into a practical policy: "They should blow up the channel tunnel and stop the buggers coming over." In the town centre, a loudspeaker is insensitively belting out *Two Tribes*.

The tram out to Hillsborough is packed and full of that cheery banter so essential for the authentic football experience. The home fans are sustained by the tanked-up defiance of one character who bangs out "Hate the Blades!" with his fist on the ceiling and shouts over and over again: "They can stab your kids, but what can they do to the Wednesday? Nothing!"

I always find Hillsborough depressing, not so much for the memory of 1989, but because the club itself never seems big enough to live comfortably in it. Certainly not now, when they are six places off the bottom of the First Division. Even for a big game like today's there are plenty of empty seats, including the two V-shaped strips in the middle of the Kop that would be the best seats in the house if they weren't right behind a pillar. Behind the scenes, though, Wednesday are still trying hard to do things in Premiership style. For one thing, they offer the press filter coffee instead of instant.

Peter Shreeves' programme notes do not inspire confidence: "My job as conductor of the orchestra is to try to bring the different qualities of the squad together. Alternatively, you could say it's like being a chef... you have all your ingredients, but there are different ways of cooking a dish." Four weeks later he will be looking for a new job in the music/food industry.

City play as if they are acting the part of a Kevin Keegan side in a film. A goal down after two minutes, they go in at half-time 2-1 up, concede an equaliser a minute after the break, then rattle in four goals in 20 minutes, swiftly raising then dashing the hopes of the man from the *Yorkshire Post*, who had loyally backed Wednesday to lose 4-2. With ten minutes to go virtually all the home fans have gone home, too shell-shocked even to boo with any conviction. I am glad not to be sharing the return journey with Mr Kid-stabber.

After about five minutes of the post-match press conferences, I start to look on managers in a completely different light. It is impossible not to feel sorry for Shreeves, even though he talks in the language of Second World War newsreels ("This was adversity with a capital A") and cannot resist the military metaphor ("Tuesday night's game is a chance to lift the troops"). More alarmingly, I find myself warming to Keegan as well. True, it is hard (even for me) to be churlish about someone whose team scores six away from home and might have had 12, but in the weeks to come I would again have to search my conscience after thanking Graeme Souness profusely for the benefit of his wisdom and wishing Trevor Francis a heartfelt good luck after his first game in charge of Crystal Palace.

"What can you tell us about Dickson Ehutu?" I ask the City manager when the initial flurry of questions has died down.

"Etuhu," he politely corrects.

Great. My public speaking debut reveals me to be one pronunciation rung below Kevin Keegan.

September 29

West Brom 1 Burnley 0

The train waits at Harrow and Wealdstone next to a sign on the platform that says "Danger, non-stop high-speed trains". For an hour and a half. The woman next to me calls someone on her mobile: "We're at Harrow and Wealdstone, wherever that is." I resist the temptation to snatch the phone from her and bellow: "It's still in flaming London, you stupid cow."

Emerging sweaty and dishevelled into the Halford's Lane Stand at five past three, after a nerve-shredding taxi ride, I can see the press box above me, but the only way to get there seems to be to push my way down a row of fans, who greet me with a selection of genial Black Country oaths, then climb over a wall that separates the reporters from the paying customers.

After that exciting but totally unprofessional entrance it's a good job the game is nothing like last week's. There is plenty of time to curse the steep angle of the desks which means the hacks are constantly clutching at pens, paper, mobiles and programmes that roll off as if on a sinking ship, note the unpretentious roll call on Albion's corporate boxes ("Traffic Signals UK", "Wormald Fire Systems") and count the number of women in the press box (one, which is one more than at Wednesday). The ground is a pleasing riot of Seventies-style yellow-and-green on three sides, and claret-and-blue on the other – less pleasing, though more authentically Seventies, is the real riot that almost breaks out at the end between the two sets of fans. Everything is right about the game – tight ground, passionate crowd – except the game itself, which never really takes off.

The press room is a small cupboard off the main concourse,

where Gary Megson and Stan Ternent stand awkwardly against the door to explain how West Brom secured the second of what would turn out to be 15 league wins by the same score in 2001-02. At Hillsborough, the managers sat up on a small stage with microphones and jugs of water, so that if you half closed your eyes you might have been waiting to hear George Bush's views on the Middle East crisis. The Hawthorns is more like a frenzied doorstep with a disgraced local councillor.

Ternent refuses to be downcast despite the blip in Burnley's bright start to the season and signs off with the one lyrical moment of the day: "Two men look through prison bars, one sees mud, one sees flowers – I'm an optimist."

November 24
Chelsea 0 Blackburn 0
My quest to see some new grounds takes me to the one I have seen only several hundred times before. Admittedly it s still a new experience, as the press box is squeezed in among the away fans on the lower tier of the East Stand, giving about the worst view I have ever had of a game at Stamford Bridge. Which really is saying something. With the reconstruction of the ground complete, the directors' box has been moved to the new West Stand, potentially leaving the prime seats on the east side free to help soothe the often fraught relations between Chelsea and the press by moving them upstairs to somewhere they can actually see the game from. Not a chance.

The game is a shocker, though Jimmy Floyd Hasselbaink does his best to lift the entertainment level by twice threatening the corner flag from a good position. He's one of those strange players, not unlike Kerry Dixon, who often looks lucky when he does something right and like a pub player when he gets it wrong. But the number of times he scores means that simply can't be true. Can it?

I am sitting next to a well-known Sunday newspaper columnist. Looking over his shoulder as he types his report with the game in progress I can make out that he has highlighted some "swift, neat passes from Zola". I check my own notes to find that I have written "scrappy", "stodgy", "boring", "pathetic" and "Did anyone tell them the players' strike was off?" in quick succession.

The crowd seem to agree with me, seeing Chelsea off with a rousing chorus of "What a load of rubbish". Although strangely, today turns out to mark the start of Rovers' decline towards the relegation zone, while Chelsea will rarely be as bad again. Afterwards Claudio Ranieri declines to appear (helping to answer the plaintive query in the programme: "Why do we get such a bad press?"), but Graeme Souness does. He is sympathetic about Ranieri's treatment by the Chelsea fans, very amiable and much shorter than he looks on TV.

December 1
Crystal Palace 1 Burnley 2
To get to the press "lounge" at Selhurst Park, you first have to get a ticket from a Portakabin in the car park. Then you go in through a turnstile, up some stairs and into a nicely appointed bar with carpets and big TVs. Only that's not for the press. So, following directions, you go down the stairs again, knock on an unmarked red door ("You're an intelligent guy, you'll find it") and ask directions in a second non-press lounge until you are finally led through the children's party area to a dingy room with some plastic cups and a bottle of Coke on a trestle table. The television is screening "Palace TV" (mostly Clinton Morrison set to music) and a sign warns of dire consequences for anyone who tries to change the channel.

This involuntary mystery tour of the Main Stand ("never one of Archibald Leitch's best" according to Simon Inglis) gives the impression it is held together with corrugated iron and bits of string. The whole place has a ramshackle, half-finished feel. The press box, perched up in the corner towards the much more impressive Holmesdale Road Stand, seems to have been knocked up in a hurry out of some leftover MDF. Random sections along the front are glazed in (or whatever the verb is when you do it with plastic), effectively distorting the view without keeping the warmth in. On the pitch, a photographer spends several minutes trying to get Pete the Eagle to imitate the steps of the chastely tracksuited pom-pom girls, but his quest for a hilarious shot is thwarted by the fact that Pete cannot hear a word he says.

It is Trevor Francis's first match in charge ("We now look forward to a stable period of progress," writes the happily deluded Simon Jordan in the programme). Francis bounces on to the pitch in shorts and a T-shirt, despite the weather, perhaps as some kind of statement. If he's been psyching the players up with tough guy rhetoric it certainly works, as Julian Gray is booked in the first minute for a lunging tackle on the visitors' Paul Weller. When the game gets going it's clear Francis has a lot of work on his hands as Palace succumb to a diligent but hardly inspired Burnley side ("We might be classed as having champagne tastes on beer money," says the ever-quotable Ternent afterwards).

My new-found tolerance for Trevor Francis possibly stems from the fact that he speaks extremely slowly – around 83 words a minute, in fact, if my almost decipherable shorthand is any guide. After hanging around for him to finish some radio interviews in the draughty and desolate stand, he gives some more time to the remaining Monday journalists. It's late and cold, his team have lost and he looks worried already, but he is polite and patient with the invariably banal questioning. This is no good at all – I'm being seduced by the cheap thrill of familiarity.

December 8

Leicester City 0 Southampton 4

Outside Leicester station there is a neat little statue of Thomas Cook, with his bags packed, umbrella in hand and (today) a carton of Ribena on his foot. It's a nice piece of work, but it gives the arriving traveller a doubtful impression of Leicester. How good can it be if their most celebrated inhabitant made his name by getting people to leave?

Walking to the ground I catch a strong whiff of cigar smoke, which can only mean one thing: Leicester Tigers are at home. Sure enough, I am quickly joined by groups of Barbour-jacketed men draped in red-white-and-green scarves that serve no practical function and middle-aged women in green felt hats. It's a relief to arrive on Almond Road, which gives on to the back-to-backs of Brazil Street. Later in the year a Millwall supporter tells me about a trip he made to Filbert Street. Losing his way, he hooked up with some other travelling fans and finally they stumbled on the same streets. "We must be nearly there," he announced, to blank looks. After he had explained the nut theme they walked on for a bit, then one of his new friends muttered to the other: "What kind of cunt knows what a filbert is anyway?"

Leicester City are a grievous loss to the Premiership, at least as far as the high-flying writers are concerned. The club is renowned for providing by far the most sumptuous spreads in the league and for the helpful and informative attitude of its press office (the food, of course, is the main thing). I am keen to savour the experience before they move to the Walkers Not-Bowl, where who knows what atrocities will be served up. It doesn't disappoint.

The press lounge is overrun with attentive officials in air steward-type uniforms. The food, legendary pasties to the fore, is magnificent (although you have to wonder what they serve upstairs in the Quorn Suite). Proper soup comes in monogrammed Leicester City bowls. Old team pictures line the walls – an obvious touch, but it reinforces the impression that City take pride in attending to detail in a way that Palace, for example, do not. On the way up to the press box you pass an impressively stocked trophy cabinet, though on closer inspection many of the larger cups seem to come from pre-season tournaments in Belgium. One states proudly (in French): "Presented by the Champion Supermarket, St Jean de Luz".

Rather than the usual free-for-all, there is a little card with your name on it taped to your desk in the press box. The voluminous notes for the media include the essential information that "cream cakes are back by popular demand at half-time". Before the game the Tannoy announcer apologises in advance for a post-punk thrash ("Maybe a bit noisy for the tastes of football supporters") which is part of the club's policy of promoting local bands.

I am sitting next to the man from the *Siam Sport Daily*, who talks animatedly in Thai on his mobile, punctuated with frequent references to Frank Sinclair. He speaks no English, except for one sentence which emerges word-perfect after Southampton's fourth: "Who put in that cross from the right?" God knows what they are making of the match in Thailand – Southampton start the day in the bottom three but Leicester, one place above, make them look like Brazil. City's new manager Dave Bassett, asked to nominate his side's best player after the match, selects "one of the subs who didn't come on".

Gordon Strachan (an exasperatingly rapid-fire 140 wpm man) talks about Anders Svensson, his £750,000 signing who has scored twice. "If he gets the winner against England I've promised him he doesn't need to do any hard running, ever." I'm reminded of this in June, when Svensson does indeed score a spectacular World Cup goal – against Argentina. Possibly one that Gordon watched with mixed feelings.

Leicester operate a proper "mixed zone", where journalists can talk to players and managers outside the confines of the formal press conference. According to the unwritten but rigidly enforced newspaper conventions, the set piece is primarily for the Sundays, while the informal mingling is where the Mondays try to glean a scrap of new material, however thin, that they can work up into a different angle. After huddling around Chris Marsden and Anders Svensson, I am pursued down a corridor by two tabloid reporters, frothing with self-righteous anger, who suspect I may be from a

Sunday, muscling in on their turf. I try to imagine what they would have done if I had admitted to gaining unauthorised insights from the softly spoken Swede – publicly burnt my notebook perhaps, or administered a swift kicking in the gents *pour encourager les autres.*

January 12
Wimbledon 0 Burnley 0
Christ. I have seen more than enough of both Burnley and Selhurst Park. It's even worse when Wimbledon are playing, particularly as the Dons fans are more concerned about their ongoing battle with chairman Charles Koppel over the move to Milton Keynes than they are with the match. Which would be understandable in any event, but even more so when the game is as poor and as inconsequential as this. My "report" is downgraded to two paragraphs as the lead item in the First Division round-up, which is just as well in one way, since there is almost nothing to say. But on the other hand, it makes you wonder what you were doing there.

Unlike Stan Ternent, I tend to see the mud rather than the flowers (in fact so does he today, describing the playing surface as "diabolical") and when I come back from a few weeks out of the country in February, I am not motivated enough to badger my superiors into putting me back on the list. A shame, though not the tragedy for me that it would have been for an ambitous, thrusting 24-year-old who wants to be the next David Lacey but one. It's a great job, but it puts you in a position which is too ambiguous to enjoy a game (or not) in the same way that you can as a fan. You are sort of working, but not really. And while you get to talk to the managers and players, you're certainly not one of them either, no matter how much some journalists would like to think so.

What have I learnt? That the rumours about Britain's train system are all true; that groups of middle-aged English men in a profession racked with suspicion tend not to talk to outsiders; that there are only so many different ways to describe a goal. And maybe that while it's interesting to see what goes on behind the scenes, you may have to pay a terrible price – the acquisition of objectivity, a willingness to see both sides of the story and the desire to be fair to everyone. Surely this cannot be what football is about.

converts' all-stars

ian farrell

Kevin Keegan may be associated with some of English football's worst failings, but the team he created at Maine Road won over the sceptics

The appointment of Joe Royle as manager, as Manchester City slid towards the Second Division in February 1998, had generally been a popular one. This was not because we were under any illusion that he was England's Johan Cruyff, but because his mixture of wit, backbone and feeling for the club instilled a measure of confidence in the hierarchy sadly missing during the Ball/Coppell/Clark/Cobbleigh years. It wasn't always pretty, but the three-year plan to get back to the top flight was achieved in two and the board's lengthy chain of bad choices seemed to have been broken.

In the euphoria that followed, the question of whether his insular brand of football was suitable for the 21st century Premiership was rarely asked. From a position of hindsight and pure logic, it might have been best to replace him at that point, but this would have been cruelly ungrateful, even for a football club, and City understandably persevered with the side that Joe had built around Alf-Inge Haaland. The consequences, both for the team and their manager, were inevitable. What we need now, they said after Royle left, is someone who'll shake things up a bit. Kick-start a new beginning. You want new beginnings kick-started? There's only one man to call. Eight months on from the ignominious end to his England reign, Kevin Keegan was back.

I'll be honest, I wasn't thrilled. In fact, I was devastated, and the reasons for this are almost as complex as the man himself. Like most, I had found his Newcastle side a breath of fresh air and his passionate honesty about the game a welcome change. His microphonic buffoonery for ITV could be annoying, of course, but more often than not I just found it funny (and infinitely preferable to the permanently irritating David Pleat). Keegan's capitulation in the psychological games with Alex Ferguson, like a weak-minded general in front of Darth Vader, was a bit embarrassing, but I wouldn't hold that against him. No, the reasons I didn't welcome the appointment run much deeper than that, and many aren't Keegan's fault. Rightly or wrongly, fairly or unfairly, he had come to represent everything I considered wrong with the English game.

Though I try to keep my self-righteous tendencies about football in check, and in particular the lack of grey matter in the British version, it's hard not to constantly bemoan the lack of sweepers and playmakers, to deride a culture where "too clever" is one of the most common insults, and an atmosphere in which moral criticism beyond the accusation of laziness is not heard. Where the most childish inability to accept not getting your own way is praised as "spirit", and where a vicious mean streak is evidence of "heart". Where expressing any sort of opinion has you marked as a troublemaker. British football is not intelligent, is not forward thinking. When it comes down to it, it's not Italian, not Dutch and not Spanish. Why should Keegan bear the brunt of this dissatisfaction? There is a one-word explanation: England.

Having lived through Bobby Robson's eight years of trench analogies and suffered through both Graham Taylor's inferiority complex and Hoddle's superiority complex, you would think that the Keegan era should not have been capable of generating such disappointment and anger. But context is everything and he was coach at a time when things were supposed to be moving forward. Hoddle, for all his other faults, had taken the international set-up onwards, while Keegan was inheriting arguably the most talented group of young players in 25 years, players who had come to the fore in the post-Wenger days of sensible diets and increased professionalism.

The circumstances were right for a genuine revival in the national team's fortunes but the manager was undeniably wrong. So wrong that it now seems unfathomably strange that he was chosen, given that the generally accepted prerequisites for a successful international manager are: 1) tactical awareness; 2) sound defensive understanding; 3) the ability to handle pressure. It is even more incredible that the FA should have been willing to go to such lengths and overcome such obstacles to get him, conferring on him the status of a saviour. OK, he was a "players' manager", in contrast to the distanced Hoddle, but what other qualities suited to the winning of international tournaments did he have?

Most of the responsibility for this lack of foresight lies at the Football Association's door. It is difficult to blame Keegan, desperate as he was to manage his country and no more blind to his own shortcomings than most of us would be to ours. My "sympathetic" attitude at the time was of the if-you-give-a-chimp-a-gun-and-it-shoots-someone-you-don't-blame-the-chimp variety. Keegan's view that foreign preparation and planning were no match for English "belief" undoubtedly set our game back, but why would anyone expect any different? Watching England throw away leads, misplace most passes over distances greater than ten yards, fail to think their way around the most primitive opposition and then trot out the worst cliches about it afterwards, one could only conclude that, though many of my complaints about British football could not be pinned on the man himself, he was nevertheless a figurehead for our arrested development. As far as I was concerned, it was time for Keegan to retire to Marbella again. When Dietmar Hamann's free-kick finally brought down the curtain on his tenure as England manager that sad, rainy day at Wembley, disappointment at the result was tempered by relief at knowing Keegan's reign of terror was over.

The question is, why City? Or, to be more suspicious, what the hell did he want with us? He is not a man who needs employment, either for financial reasons or because of an overwhelming addiction to the game. A likely reason may well have been to rescue a reputation bruised by an England failure which was partly obscured by press bonhomie and player "respect", but nevertheless comparable to Graham Taylor's. This was not a strong enough reason to take just any job. For it to be of any interest to Keegan it needs to be a "project", with the words "ambition" and "potential" never far from the conversation.

And yet, compared to his previous club environments, City are profoundly unambitious. At Newcastle, he lived with John Hall's dreams of creating a Geordie Barcelona, a sporting giant defending and defining a region and its people. Likewise, the grand plans of Mohamed al-Fayed appealed to Keegan the dreamer. By contrast, City chairman David Bernstein does not seem burdened by quite such lofty aspirations. For the first time Keegan isn't backed by a man with the psychological profile of a Bond villain.

The press releases and the interviews and the cheerleaders who call phone-in shows all told me of the revolution to come. I wasn't wholly convinced by this romantic notion of Keegan the wandering revolutionary, a shell-suited Che Guevara ushering in a radical new regime. A shift from defending recklessly to attacking recklessly did not strike me as much of a development. And could he match Joe's natural touch with the post-match quip? The Keegan philosophy is all about going forward. It struck me as a move sideways.

Unavoidably, there were comparisons with the Newcastle of

1992, mostly involving the phrase "sleeping giant", but they were largely erroneous. Newcastle at the time were a crumbling, money-losing ruin, playing in front of small crowds and operating out of run-down facilities. By contrast, City had a squad of recent Premiership players, a sound and sensible board and 32,000 regular fans, a figure soon to become 45,000 at a new stadium. The answer to why Keegan chose Manchester City could well be down to his age. He may have the same destination as his Newcastle adventure in mind but, now in his fifties, he'd prefer to start the journey a bit further down the road.

But we're getting ahead of ourselves. First, there was the little matter of navigating a path out of the First Division. The general expectation, with an up-and-down coach taking charge of a team changing divisions for the fourth time in five summers, was of a rollercoaster ride. All heart no head, able to switch easily between the sublime and the chaotic. Expect the unexpected.

Though I was by no means in the majority in my dissatisfaction, there were plenty who were, shall we say, waiting to be won over. Those hoping to be bribed by big name signings were to be initially disappointed and should not have expected anything else. The Keegan way has always been to buy at times of strength, enabling your club to attract a better class of player and putting you in a better bargaining position, whereas going into the market in desperation is an invitation to get shafted. Sure enough, he added only the grit of Stuart Pearce and the guile of Eyal Berkovic in the close season. More would come later, when the club was near or at the top.

The campaign started in accordance with those expectations of inconsistency – comfortable victories followed by the odd 4-0 hammering. The pundits nodded their heads in quiet satisfaction, but they were to be proved wrong. A humiliation at home by Wimbledon in October marked a turning point and from then on it was one long march to the title. City weren't totally bullet-proof, losing seven more matches in all competitions, but all were by a single goal and all were away from Maine Road. They did all the things champions are supposed to do – blowing away opponents with attacking par excellence most weeks, playing poorly but jammily grinding it out for the same reward the rest. Everyone had expected a nerve-jangling adventure, but, apart from an admirable refusal to join in the bullying of Stockport, the team was marked from the autumn onwards by a machine-like consistency.

The upturn happened, not coincidentally, around the time of Ali Bernarbia's arrival, easily the most important of the mid-season signings. The club that had struggled to find a consistent place for Georgi Kinkladze now had two playmakers, as the Algerian complemented rather than replaced Berkovic. (The Arab and the Israeli in perfect harmony – if only the world was more like a Keegan midfield.) The team was playing the best football in the division, arguably the best outside the Premiership's top five, and it certainly wasn't down to a reckless, attack-crazy approach either – maybe it was the context of Nationwide League football, but the side looked very well organised.

Not only was Keegan winning me over with the football, but also with his performances in the media arena. Away from the spotlight and the banner headlines, he seemed a quieter, more reflective man. Yes, he could still be a bit of a berk, but who can't? All that stuff about his enthusiasm and his ability to stimulate it in others that I had previously sneered at suddenly meant something to me. His passionate oratory was no longer refracted through tabloid hidden agendas and I could accept his words for what they were: honest feelings from a man who cares.

Any hope that he could continue his rehabilitation by staying out of the spotlight all season were dashed by the FA Cup. First, a big win at Ipswich, but that was nothing compared to the tie it earned them: Newcastle away. Worries that this might cause a regression to his earlier Colemanballs-friendly incarnation were quickly extinguished. Yes, it was an emotional return and his feelings were reciprocated by a grateful crowd, but in many ways it was just another game to be won. The heart was on the sleeve to some degree, but it was easily overruled by a head more concerned with replacing the suspended Bernarbia and showing the watching TV audience that City were to be taken seriously. Five years is a long time.

Things were changing for certain and not just on the pitch. Rumours abounded of behind-the-scenes alterations too. He had brought in two trusted assistants: the semi-invisible Derek Fazackerley and the semi-legendary Arthur Cox, as loyal and intimidating as a Cosa Nostra leg-breaker. The pair were the manager's eyes and ears and kept tabs on just about everything. People began to speak of a fanatical attention to detail: everything had to be right. Royle and his predecessors, unfairly or not, had lived with accusations of organisational unprofessionalism. This, it seems, is not the Keegan way. I was warming to him by the day.

Naturally all this pleased me, but it put me in a difficult position. I had always railed against hypocritical opinion-revising when a previously hated figure joins your club – when vicious bastards become "100 per centers" and cheating scumbags are suddenly "clever" and "professional" – and yet here I was, a self-appointed opponent of Keegan, starting to sing his praises as the club sat on top of the division. True, this was only because he was at Maine Road, but my new-found feelings of respect were genuine. He was admirably honest in assessing his own failings with the England team, but they did not make him a bad manager, just a bad international manager. Club football is a very different animal and I had to admit that he knew what he was doing.

During a pub argument I even put forward a theory inconceivable a year earlier: Kevin Keegan is, in fact, England's Cruyff. When sanity returned the next morning I recanted of course (although with City's disregard for coaching orthodoxy and lack of interest in defending I could see where I was coming from), but the fact that I would say this in any mental state highlights just how much my views had changed. For most people, the Cruyff analogy falls down on the difference in intelligence between the two (though I would prefer to concentrate on the fact that Keegan does not share Cruyff's arrogance). In one corner the Einstein of football, in the other a man who distrusts all that fancy book learnin' on the grounds that Bill Shankly never needed it. There is a good deal of truth in these descriptions , but the image of Keegan as the tactical troglodyte, filling up many a web page with his mixed metaphors and bizarre pronouncements, is nevertheless a slightly unfair distortion. This may seem like a very small compliment, but there are plenty of people in football who are far more stupid.

So, how do I feel now the new era is up and running? I would consider myself a convert and a partial fan. I am not blind to his faults, but unlike my former comrades who cannot see past the walkouts, the Sky interview breakdown and the ridiculous sayings, I can appreciate his many qualities. By the time you read this, Bernstein may have withdrawn a promised transfer kitty to prompt a resignation, but I doubt it. Keegan seems happy at Maine Road, and we're very happy to have him. Francis Lee was to be a saviour. Successive managers were, we were told, just what this club needs. The Kappa kit deal was supposed to be the start of something.

Now, though, after too many false starts, City have a real chance to make a leap forward and leave the pantomime of the 1990s well and truly behind. A new stadium is coming. A sensible, decent chairman is willing to back a talented, dedicated coach he believes in. No one is making five-year plans culminating in winning the Champions League (or if they are they're not talking about it), but there is a feeling that City can become, well, normal. Sane. And we have Kevin Keegan to thank for it.

The last word goes not to Shankly, to whom Keegan's devotion is well documented, but to a lesser-known influence: the great American football coach Vince Lombardi. Lombardi, whose teachings have become standard motivational reading in many walks of life, was of the "winning isn't everything, it's the only thing" school. This may be difficult to reconcile with the traditional image of Keegan, but Lombardi wasn't totally ruthless. Like Shankly and his pupil, he had an innate sense of decency and a belief that you should win within the rules. He also recognised that "loser" isn't always an insult and Keegan would no doubt pick a quote of his as an obituary for his time at Newcastle and a rebuttal of his critics: "In great attempts, it is glorious even to fail." One long year on from my initial horror, I am hoping he's more mindful of another Lombardi aphorism: "Once you learn to quit, it becomes a habit." Things change.

taking the michel

john chapman

It was business as usual for Belgium's perennial under-achievers Standard Liège: a chaotic mess caused by doubtful characters sticking their oar in

Liège is an agreeable place to spend a weekend. You can walk in the footsteps of one of its most famous sons, Georges Simenon, and have a beer or two in one of the cafes where Maigret's creator found his first inspiration. It was Simenon who said: "Writing is not a profession but a vocation of unhappiness." Something similar might be said of being a Standard Liège supporter. It is now ten years since the club won the Belgian cup and 20 years since they were champions. That's far too long for a club that believes only Anderlecht can challenge its right to be Belgium's top dog.

With hindsight, then, 2001-02 was a fairly typical season at Sclessin. With local hero Michel Preud'homme in charge of team affairs, the campaign began promisingly, moved into top gear at the halfway stage – with talk of the championship coming home – only to descend into panto-like farce during the run-in. Standard Liège being the club it is, however, this one is set to run and run. After the championship had once again escaped them, the men in suits contacted national coach Robert Waseige and got him to sign on the dotted line, just as the Belgium squad left for Japan. Now the talk is of glory in the coming season. Yeah, right.

The pivotal point of the season was a spell at a training camp at Knokke, Belgium's answer to Brighton, just after the mid-season winter break. With his side in joint top spot, Preud'homme had announced that Liège could win the championship. We're talking hostages and fortunes here. From that moment, it was all downhill. At the camp, administrative director general Alphonse Constantin, also known as "the Sheriff" and occasionally "Adolf", told leading scorer Ali Lukunku that the club had been wrong to give him a new contract lasting until 2006. Lukunku's form subsequently dipped alarmingly.

Club captain Didier Ernst, the team's engine and one of the most popular players at Sclessin, was approaching the end of his own contract. Ernst didn't like the new terms on offer. "I'm a Standard man through and through, but if they do nothing to keep me, I'll draw my own conclusions," he said. Later, Ernst described the new terms as "a typical Liège increase – the same salary but they take away your car".

But the board of directors were not satisfied with merely unsettling two key players. They needed another destructive assault on the team's spirit. A few weeks later, they found it. Each player was given a target weight. Anyone failing to meet it would be fined £350 per excess kilo. Even better, the results could then be leaked to the press. Lukunku, recovering from injury, duly found that his monthly pay check was lighter, as did six other players, including Belgium internationals Michael "Mika" Goossens and Eric van Meir. The centre-back saw the funny side: "No one said anything, not even Constantin, when we beat Ghent and Bruges and I was the same weight then." The BBC heard about the story and sent a team over to Belgium but no one at Liège was available for comment.

Standard Liège is not an ordinary club. The president is a Swiss hotel owner, Reto Stiffler, who is hardly ever seen. "Alf II" (it works in French) Constantin runs everything at Sclessin except the team, where Preud'homme is nominally in charge. The club's website has a handy chart showing the positions of all its staff, but the name of the real Mr Big does not appear there. That man is Luciano d'Onofrio, friend of the famous, who claims to earn his keep through players such as Zinedine Zidane rather than Standard Liège. D'Onofrio is officially an "advisor" to Liège. The club is a hobby, albeit an expensive one. He is said to have invested several million pounds in Liège and will probably be looking for a return.

D'Onofrio is also a FIFA-registered agent, working out of Portugal, and is generally reckoned to have been the man behind Zidane's move from Bordeaux to Juventus. He has a number of players on his books, including the Mpenza brothers, Emile and Mbo, who both gained expensive transfers from Liège in the Nineties. One more name on the Liège website, and organisation chart, is Robert Louis-Dreyfus (RLD). Louis-Dreyfus is a very rich man indeed. His CV includes periods of employment with Saatchi & Saatchi and Adidas, where he was chief executive officer. He's pumped millions of pounds into Marseille and is a major shareholder at Liège.

Since Louis-Dreyfus and d'Onofrio have been involved, a steady stream of players has moved from Liège to Marseille. So far Belgium's World Cup centre-back Daniel van Buyten (touted as the new Jaap Stam), the outstanding Nigerian full-back Joseph Yobo and Croat keeper Vedran Runje have all made the journey. Van Buyten and Yobo were later linked with Juventus, where d'Onofrio has excellent contacts, although Yobo ended up at Goodison Park. (Sometimes fairy tales don't have a happy ending.) Any profits on such moves are shared 50-50 between Liège and Marseille.

Locally, however, Constantin is always depicted as the villain of the piece. He has a habit of giving interviews in the third person.

"Constantin refuses to criticise his predecessors but he found a lot of problems when he arrived at the club," is a typical comment. Despite heart surgery, the 56-year-old works six days a week at Liège, from 6am to 8pm. Then he goes jogging. When the club were at Knokke, Constantin arrived on the beach in a brand new tracksuit and told the players that he was going to surprise a few players, as he regularly jogged 25 miles per week. After a few minutes, Constantin was already 200 metres behind the squad. Observers noticed that the pace seemed to be appreciably faster than usual.

Later, giving a farewell interview to *Foot* magazine, Ernst described the former referee as "a clown" and "the messenger boy". The ex-captain, hoping for a move to the Bundesliga, added: "If d'Onofrio asked Constantin to jump in the [river] Meuse, he'd do it immediately." Unsurprisingly, results were poor in the aftermath of the Knokke camp trip and injuries became more and more frequent. Preud'homme was criticised for being too gentle with players. Some of them even greeted him with a kiss (as is the Belgian way) in the mornings. As Ernst said: "There's nothing wrong with that but where players are in competition, it begins to look like favouritism." The former international keeper is also pretty laid-back. Ernst added that when you see Preud'homme's assistant going absolutely crazy on the bench, you begin to wonder who is in charge. Preud'homme's assistant is d'Onofrio's brother, Dominique.

A legendary keeper for Belgium and Liège, Preud'homme returned to the club 18 months ago in a blaze of publicity. Joining in mid-season, he took the club to third place and into Europe for the first time in six years. Initially he sought to be friends with everyone. Good results followed and he settled on a 4-3-3 formation with the Portuguese flyer Almani Da Silva Moreira, Lukunku and Goossens up front. But Preud'homme wasn't helped by the composition of his technical staff. An unnamed source said that he was being helped by a swimming instructor and a car mechanic. The coach later showed that he had retained a sense of humour by retorting that every club should have a swimming instructor and a car mechanic on its staff.

In the aftermath of Knokke, Ernst was axed from the team. His failure to agree a new contract had cost him his place. He wasn't pleased. "Preud'homme wanted to keep me, but the management had decided I no longer existed. The coach said I was only thinking about a transfer, but it was d'Onofrio talking really." Goossens and Lukunku were permanently on the treatment table. That made team selection easier, but Preud'homme found himself short of players. Enter d'Onofrio, who happened to have a couple of players languishing in foreign parts: the former Belgium international full-back (and one-time Coventry City player) Regis Genaux at Udinese and Croatian international Robert Spehar at Galatasary. Both had hardly played in years but they were on d'Onofrio's books and it would be good business for everyone if they succeeded.

They didn't. The injury-prone Genaux hardly got a game and, embarrassingly, was left on the bench after four games because if he played five he would have received a bonus. Spehar had been a scoring sensation at Bruges in the Nineties but that was now a distant memory. In ten appearances he scored three goals and disappeared from the scene. Team spirit, such as it was, evaporated and Europe became a distant dream. Lukunku had had enough and was brave enough to speak out. The French-Congolese striker has had a chequered career at Liège since joining from Monaco in 1998. He became the butt of a hostile crowd, having a brick thrown through his window and the tyres slashed on his car. Shouts of "Go back to where you came from" were common. During this time, friends told him not to read internet forums, for fear of what he would see there. Racism is certainly alive and well in parts of Liège.

But Lukunku didn't run away. Famously, his old coach Tomislav Ivic had once sent him on as a substitute with the words: "We're both in the shit Ali, do it for me." Lukunku did, leaving the bench to score a winning goal. Later, he was voted player of the season.

Lukunku remains laconic, insisting that "overall, Liège has good fans". Instead, the player reserved his criticism for Constantin. According to Lukunku, Constantin told him that the technical staff no longer wanted him. Yet this was only a few months after Anderlecht had offered £2 million for the striker. Liège asked for twice as much and the deal folded. But it was more personal than that. Lukunku had tried to talk to Constantin one lunchtime about a fine that had been imposed on him for no apparent reason. According to Lukunku, Constantin answered: "I'm eating. Go and talk to people of your own level." For that incident, Lukunku received another £350 fine for showing a lack of respect to Constantin.

Lukunku had also been fined for being overweight. He decided to shape up and went to a professional dietician. Back at Liège, he was forced to eat the same as everyone else. For his outburst in *Foot*, Lukunku was fined again – £800 this time. "At the end of the season, I'll hire a lawyer to get the fines back," he said. "It's not in my contract that I have to weigh less than 90 kilos and show excessive respect to Constantin."

Goossens is another interesting character. He made his debut for Liège as a teenager but joined Schalke 04 in 1997, only to return three years later. Goossens is a genuine local hero, having once been a member of the notorious "Hell Side" fans, whose support for the team can often manifest itself in the hurling of seats on to pitches at opposing grounds. Last season, there was an outbreak of thefts in the dressing room and Goossens was immediately in the frame. He was in charge of the team kitty, which also went missing. Goossens was accused of giving it to the Hell Side. "Do they think I'm mad?" he said. Goossens claims that he himself lost personal effects, including clothes, toiletries and football kit. Constantin then claimed to have received death threats on his mobile phone. The usual suspect was rounded up. Goossens offered to help if Constantin told him the numbers of the people making the threats. There was no follow-up.

Finally, there were rumours of a demonstration against the club by the Hell Side crew. D'Onofrio got involved. On the assumption that Goossens knew the leaders of the protest, he said to Goossens: "If there's one banner protesting against us on the kop, you'll never play football again." In this climate, it was hardly surprising that results were not exactly going Liège's way. Something had to give and before the end of the season it did – Preud'homme. The coach announced that he would be made technical director in 2002-03 and that the hunt was on for a replacement.

D'Onofrio played a clever game to the end. He said that the decision was Preud'homme's alone and that his own preference had been for him to stay as coach. D'Onofrio also damned Preud'homme with faint praise, arguing that he had merely built on the work of Ivic. The players who have spoken out have not been forgotten. D'Onofrio said that Preud'homme's tactics of treating everyone equally would have worked with professionals but not with a group that included "*sales gamins*" (dirty urchins). Ernst's Liège career is over, while Lukunku and Goossens are living on borrowed time. Goossens' case is more interesting – his agent is Luciano d'Onofrio.

After weeks of speculation and denial from the man himself, the 62-year-old Robert Waseige agreed to become Liège's coach – for the third time. So Preud'homme will find himself the line manager of the man who introduced him to the first division, 25 years ago. Preud'homme says he wants to run Liège along the lines of Alex Ferguson at Old Trafford, but he may well find himself between a rock and a hard place. Waseige and d'Onofrio go back a long, long way, having grown up in Liège together. This could be the continuation of a beautiful friendship.

surplus valois

neil rose

Luton's new French signing was brilliant and they went up in record-breaking style. Unfortunately, the two weren't really connected

Of the many foreigners to pass through the doors of Kenilworth Road in recent times, my favourite – until last season – was Johnny Vilstrup from Denmark. This was because when he joined Luton Town in 1995, he came equipped with the most fantastic, Hot Shot Hamish-style claim to fame: he possessed, we were assured, the hardest shot in Danish football. Given the generally hearty, healthy ways of Scandinavians, we presumed that he had to hit the ball pretty damn hard to gain that accolade. We wondered if there were competitions on Danish television to determine who had the hardest shot, on which, to national acclaim, it was Johnny who ripped the net from the frame with a ferocious strike.

Vilstrup was one of a clutch of players brought in by Terry Westley, who had been promoted from youth team coach to manager in the summer after David Pleat had once again upped sticks. Sadly, the Dane proceeded to trundle around the pitch to no great effect and his career at Luton came to an abrupt halt not long after Westley was booted out in November 1995 with the team firmly rooted in the bottom three of the First Division. Johnny singularly failed to prove that he could shoot at all, let alone shoot harder than anyone else in Denmark – although I have a vague memory that could well be entirely made up of one bazooka-like effort that left the crossbar oscillating – and new boss Lennie Lawrence waved him off without shedding much of a tear or probably even learning his name.

Having arrived from obscurity, Vilstrup quickly returned there – assuming that a few months at the bottom of the First Division counts as visibility – although in 1996 he did win a Danish Cup winner's medal with AGF of Aarhus, in a side that also included Torben Piechnik, Havard Flo and Stig Tofting (who was voted "Cup fighter of the year").

The basic moral of Johnny Vilstrup's tale is that, by and large, foreign players have not taken too well to the verdant hills of Bedfordshire, the historic postwar architecture of downtown Luton and the dizzying shopping carnival that is the Arndale. Until the 2001-02 season, that is. After a decade of steady and depressing decline, we were back down in the bottom division for the first time in more than 30 years. Indeed, Luton had now become the first team to have twice made the journey from bottom division to top and back again.

Joe Kinnear had declared publicly that if he failed to win promotion he should be sacked, and those fans still suspicious of his Wimbledon heritage were all too ready to clear his desk for him. Backed by a wealthy chairman and aware that the squad he inherited would struggle to give the Luton Belles junior team much of a game, Kinnear threw the cash around, mainly picking up Bosmans and paying up the contracts of those he wanted out. Only three regulars from the year before made it into the line-up.

The team made a good start and then, in September, came Jean-Louis Valois. There is no better way to describe him than as a poor man's David Ginola: a mecurial Frenchman blessed with outrageous skill, a questionable work ethic, flowing locks, a sweet left foot and a reluctance to track back, who, as a result, was intimately acquainted with the bench.

We'd been down this road once before and, frankly, we were sceptical. In 1998, a former Monaco striker called Hervé Bacqué popped up out of nowhere, scored a couple of terrific goals in pre-season friendlies against Arsenal and Coventry and led us to believe that we had ourselves our very own Eric Cantona. Sadly, once the real action began, Hervé proved himself nothing more than the beach footballer Eric subsequently became, and his nine goalless games for the club came to an ignominious end during a 3-0 home drubbing by Walsall in the Auto Windscreens, when he buggered up a penalty.

Valois was signed from Lens – that was, to our amazement, the same Lens that played in the French first division. He had even – get this – played in the Champions League. Even though he had become a squad player in recent times, it seemed rather a long way down and there was much muttering that he would prefer to be playing for a bigger team. After all, he had once had a trial at Preston. But he was quickly seduced by the glamour of his new surroundings, making his debut in a home game against Torquay.

It was unendingly, unbelievably, unmatchably glorious. From the first impudent flick and outrageous shuffle which left a defender gawping at thin air like a cartoon character who's run off the edge of a cliff but takes a moment to understand his predicament, Valois was the kind of player who, as the cliche has it, you would pay the entrance money just to see. He ignored his theoretical station on the left wing and roamed far and wide across the Torquay half of the pitch. They didn't have the slightest idea what to do about him.

The soaring left-foot cross from the right which landed on Carl Griffiths' head at the end of the first half and flew into the net was just one example of what he was capable of. Griffiths scored a hat-trick of top-quality headers, but he was nothing more than a sideshow that day as the Hatters ran out 5-1 winners. Good heavens, Valois could even put a corner or a free-kick exactly where it was meant to go. Had nobody told him this was the Third Division? Home of the lumbering centre-back, journeyman winger and honest, if skill-free, endeavour?

The second half brought one of those rare footballing moments when you feel a thrill course through you and the roar of delight issues from the pit of your stomach. Valois cut in from the left and, with minimal backlift, fired a bullet from 35 yards. The keeper flailed with pleasing futility as it rushed past him into the far top corner. It was so good that everyone in the crowd looked at each other and just laughed. The draught caused by all the disbelieving, shaking heads developed into a hurricane by the time it reached China, so I'm told.

Valois is a born showman and, with impeccable timing, left the field with cramp about ten minutes from the end. The entire ground rose in appreciation, little guessing that in the months to come the rest of his early exits would be involuntary. Never had a player made such an impact in his first match. Forget the fact that this was Torquay at home – he was truly stupendous. It then turned out that, contrary to reports, Kinnear hadn't actually signed the Frenchman. Panic ensued. Sir Alex would be on the phone within minutes. However, 24 hours later, Valois had put his name to a contract until the end of the season. Promotion was surely guaranteed with this wizard in our ranks.

Luton have enjoyed their fair share of entertainers over the years, and so we gloried in Valois' skill. But like most clubs, for every Ricky Hill and David Moss we have had to endure countless Darren McDonoughs and Chris Kamaras, the sort of player for whom the ball is an optional extra and who seems genetically driven to commit a foul every four minutes (I once timed Kamara and it was his sixth foul on the 24-minute mark that brought the booking). A propos of nothing, I was arguably the first person to see Kevin Keegan's shortcomings as a manager: any man who made McDonough his first signing in an effort to kickstart a revolution – as Keegan did at Newcastle – showed their judgment was almost as questionable as the chap from Decca Records who told the fledgling Beatles that guitar music was on the way out.

Yet we hadn't seen anything quite like Valois. How would he cope, we wondered with a traditional mistrust of foreign players, on a chilly evening at Orient? Rather well, came the reply four days later, as he waltzed past a couple of defenders and smashed it in from a mere 25 yards, this time with his right foot. A two-footed footballer? Whatever next? More than 2,000 away fans exulted.

Valois couldn't repeat the magic next time out, and was substituted in a crunch game at Plymouth, which we lost despite having a man advantage for more than a half. But back at Kenilworth Road six days later it was Torquay all over again, with Valois playing a starring role in a 5-2 Friday night demolition of Darlington. He capped a bravura performance which included a near copycat 35-yard piledriver into the top corner (again with his right foot) with a breakaway from a Darlington corner in the dying minutes, when he slalomed his way 70-odd yards, only to be fouled in the act of finishing it off. Despite the cries of the crowd and the demands of natural justice, he was denied the opportunity to take the penalty himself (which was missed). He probably would have backheeled it in while bowing to the fans.

All was sweetness and light. We were top of the table and the club's website made jokey references to JLV's inability to speak any English, let alone training ground English, and how this led to hilarious mix-ups with Joe Kinnear over his demands that crosses reach the back stick. The media paid him some attention, and so, soon afterwards, did a legion of right-backs and doubling-up right-sided midfielders.

It was inevitable that he couldn't keep it up and, gradually, a slight air of disappointment began to embrace Valois. For me, it started with the fans' decision to dispense with the obvious and uplifting chant – a Cantona-style "Oooh aaah Val-er-ois" etc – and instead go for "Jean-Louis Val-er-ois" to the tune of *La Donna e Mobile*. I admit I don't know much about opera, but I could have sworn that was an Italian ditty.

Then came the realisation – and this took several months of fitfully sparkling performances down the wing – that JLV was a good man to have on your side when things were going well, but something of a luxury when they weren't. This was disappointingly standard behaviour for a flair player, and was presumably why such a talent was stuck in our division. I felt let down. Surely Jean-Louis was more than just a stereotype?

Sadly, the answer appeared to be no. The jinks and quick feet were still there, providing a bewitching ability to conjure an escape from aggressive markers, and there were still many flashes of dazzling skill, but slowly the crosses and set-pieces became less pinpoint, the runs less effective, the irritation at his unwillingness to tackle back more pronounced. The captain Kevin Nicholls, a box-to-box, run-through-a-brick-wall-at-your-command sort, was clearly less than impressed by this last aspect of JLV's game.

Kinnear discovered a highly effective tactic to shake things up at half-time. Valois would come off and be replaced by a defender who would go to left-back, releasing Matthew Taylor up the wing. Taylor – young, hugely energetic, prodigiously talented and possessor of a cracking left foot – took his chance greedily. He gave Town a very direct drive up the flank that Valois didn't, and an ability to get to the far post for crosses from the right that Valois would never bother with. Goals – 11 in all – and assists came for the youngster, as did the scouts. Where originally they may have been casting their eye over this French sensation they'd heard about, now Taylor was the target.

There were several exceptions. Leaders Plymouth came to Kenilworth Road protecting a seven-point lead and left with their tails between their legs and a well-deserved 2-0 beating, orchestrated by

Valois. There was also talk of injury hampering the Frenchman, but the suspicion persisted that this was a smokescreen which allowed Kinnear to drop and substitute an established fan favourite.

Come mid-February and Luton were wobbling slightly. Despite having been in the top three for virtually the whole season and scoring goals aplenty, we lost three games out of four and the pack was closing in. But a couple of judicious signings finally sorted out an erratic defence, and Luton went on a stunning run that saw us win 13 and draw one of our last 14 games, scoring 35 and conceding just six. It may be harsh on Jean-Louis to note this, but he was largely a peripheral figure in the run, finishing just one of the 11 games he started in that spell.

As promotion became a certainty and the weather improved, Valois' form picked up, and he even scored a couple of nice goals during the run-in, albeit from the less challenging distances of six and 12 yards respectively. When he was good, he was very, very good, and when he was bad, he was... well, not horrid, just ineffective. In some ways, I blame English football. Being at a level like the Third Division and under a very traditional English manager like Kinnear, Valois was eventually forced to do things on the pitch he had probably heard about but never considered as part of his role: sticking to his position, tackling back and tracking forward runs, to name but three. I sometimes had a sense that we were slowly strangling what made him such a wonder.

Luton's hugely entertaining season finished with 98 goals, 97 points and 96 bookings. Club records were shattered, most notably through a whopping 15 away wins. This all put Luton second behind a Plymouth team without our flair but with the defensive solidity we had lacked for two-thirds of the campaign. Irritating, really; any other season in recent years and 97 points would have run away with the title, but this time we had to make do with the promotion promised nine months earlier. Ever the gent, Kinnear grumbled that Plymouth was good for fish and chips, and dying in, but nothing more.

All the indications were that Jean-Louis Valois would return from whence he came, along with a girlfriend who couldn't settle in the UK. His star would have burnt briefly but astonishingly brightly, and while he hadn't quite scaled the Olympian heights of those heady first few weeks again, we would thank him for those memories alone. At least, unlike Johnny Vilstrup, we would remember him for something he had done gloriously, rather than a glorious something he probably hadn't done and showed no ability to do.

And then the surprise in June: Valois was putting pen to paper for another two years. A month later though, with a characteristic body swerve, he wasn't. Suddenly, he was training with Rotherham, only to fulfil his ambition for higher level football by ultimately signing for Hearts. Watching on jealously as he played a major role in their early games, I thought of all those Scottish fans whose jaws would be dropping like ours did last year. It won't be long, I can tell them that now, but it'll be great while it lasts.

# of arses and buckets

matt nation

Holger Stanislawski embodied the uniquely earthy traditions of his club. But no one else was quite traditional enough to share them

One of the drawbacks of the ageing of the planet is that we are confronted with an ever-increasing number of predecessors: there are more and more former colleagues who didn't leave coffee stains on their desk and who used to bring in cake on their birthday; there are more and more former partners of current partners who "weren't better and weren't worse, just... different", with the three dots getting longer each time. There is more and more of everyone able to do more and more of everything. It must have been excellent being Adam, or Eve, or a stegosaurus, or anybody without a forerunner. You wonder if they knew just how good they had it.

In the case of football teams, there is almost always one predecessor who will cast shadows over their club forever more. Peter Schmeichel once famously suggested that the Manchester United team of 1999 would have hammered the 1968 team out of sight, and he was probably right. Yet it is the latter that will always be remembered more fondly. For FC St Pauli, the predecessor never to be emulated is the promotion team of 1988. Even if a St Pauli side of the future managed to win every domestic trophy for the rest of time, the general consensus would still prevent them from holding a candle to the team of 14 years ago. Just like the people who claim to have been at the forefront of the punk movement, when their birth certificates say they would just have been leaving primary school, there are 15-year-old St Pauli supporters who still fondly recall Ralf Sievers' winning goal against Bayern Munich in 1991.

In 1988, Holger Stanislawski, the long-serving captain of the current St Pauli team, would have been in his late teens. He might not have been a St Pauli supporter – most people in Hamburg aren't, particularly if they spend several months playing in the youth team at arch-rivals Hamburger SV, as Stani did – but, as a native Hamburger, he can't have failed to notice the euphoria that swept through the city. The supporters were different, the team was a ragtag bunch of anti-stars. And he probably wanted to be part of it.

As regards playing ability, Stani dovetailed with St Pauli "like an arse on a bucket", as they say in these parts, and as Stani would almost certainly have said himself. Stani played every match as though it were just one great big game of British Bulldog on grass. So-called experts praised his heading ability, but even that was little more than average – after all, he was a defender. Defenders are expected to be good in the air and, with the exception of the exceptional – Moore, Beckenbauer, Neville – they always are. But Stani's greatest asset was simply his willingness to get stuck in. In fact, he didn't even appear to like the ball very much at all. Even today, from the back row of the terraces, you can see Stani's look of slight exasperation whenever the ball comes to him, almost as though it should have learnt its lesson by now. In Stani's book, you concentrate on your strengths and pretend your weaknesses don't exist.

More significant than his eye for a scrap, at least from a press point of view, were Stani's northern German roots. Regional pride is taken very seriously indeed throughout Germany. Blood groups aren't defined by letters, but by postal districts. A friend of mine from the Wiedenbrück part of Rheda-Wiedenbrück, a small town in Westphalia, regularly works himself into a frenzy about the fact that his district comes after, rather than before, the hyphen in his town's name.

North Germans, if not as irascible, are just as passionate about their region. The climate, wretched for ten months of the year, is viewed not as a reason to be perpetually miserable, but as a gilt-edged opportunity to go for walks in your new sou'wester. Countryside with the relief and points of interest of an ironing board is not considered a reason to live in constant fear of flooding, but as a chance to develop an extra-special relationship with the sky. Pickled herrings are not the sort of things you eat just before, or just after, a hangover, but the "sushi of the western world". The fact that not all players from other regions of Germany would prefer to come and live in Wolfsburg over, say, anywhere else, is perhaps understandable. However, the problem with north Germany in general, and Hamburg in particular, is that, in recent years, they've had problems retaining their home-grown stars as well.

Andreas Brehme, ultimately responsible for winning West Germany the World Cup in 1990, left Hamburg in the midst of Keeganmania for the relative tranquillity of Kaiserslautern. Stefan Effenberg, the most gifted player ever to stand around in the centre circle and slow down a promising move by playing a square pass, left his home town without ever turning out even for a top amateur side, and finds it difficult to conceal his disdain for his birthplace whenever interviewed on returning for an away game. (Natives of Hamburg have long since ceased to regard this as a personal affront, seeing as Effenberg treats anybody with disdain who isn't staring back at him from a mirror.) Even Oliver Bierhoff, although not a native of Hamburg, spent time at HSV before being dismissed as a one-trick pony (the fact that this trick seems to be maintaining a goal-every-other-game ratio at international level clearly wasn't enough for the men in charge).

But those are the good players. In a city of nigh-on two million inhabitants, the not-so-good players are available in abundance. In the 1988 promotion season, not one of the not-so-good St Pauli players (which was all of them) appeared to have been born south of the Elb. Jürgen Gronau, a stalwart midfielder whose loyalty to the club remained unwavering for more than 20 years, was regularly asked why he stayed faithful. His reply – "Nobody else wants me" – should be incorporated into the club crest. It seemed all you needed to do was boast a working knowledge of the local Low German dialect (which basically consists of noises that you would make after eating unbuttered sandwiches too quickly) and they'd give you a game.

Stani had that as well. He not only looked like somebody trying to sell bags of bananas at the fish market of a Sunday morning, he also had the plodding accent, the sort where his conversational partners interrupt him in mid-sentence because they think he's finished what he wants to say. Stani was more north German than all the marinated seafood, drainage ditches and fictitious maritime backgrounds you could care to think of.

And Stani wanted to be loved. He even admitted as much in public. In an interview shortly after he had arrived at the club, Stani was asked what he'd like to achieve in his career. Instead of mentioning trophies, contracts and having a daughter called Chloe and a son called Sam, Stani simply expressed the wish that his name be chanted from the terraces. "Stani. Stani. Two syllables. It's really easy. Anybody can do it." Even the most hard-bitten cynic recognised instantly that this wasn't the preening of a self-professed dressing-room guv'nor; Stani wanted the comic-strip dream. He wanted echoes, he wanted jagged speech bubbles with his name surrounded by crotchets and minims. Even though it was never going to happen.

Holger Stanislawski didn't have the alliteration of a Horst Hrubesch or, indeed, of a Kevin Keegan. Besides, there was the fact that he was playing in the same team as Martino Gatti, owner of a perfect five-syllable arrangement for terrace chanting. And then there were also the supporters, who were too busy off on tangents singing about "Gyros, tsatziki and a side salad as well" (origins unknown) or "Göbel and riff-raff" (in deference to a juggernaut of a centre-forward who used to smash up his opponents) to bother themselves with a trifling double-syllable surname. But he carried hope in his heart and wore his heart on his sleeve, and there was no one, man woman or child who, on reading the interview, didn't want to stand in front of him, arms outstretched and say: "Come here, you big old daft a'porth, just come here."

So when St Pauli went up in 2000, it was Stani's promotion as much as anybody else's. Stani had been a member of the team that went up in 1995, but it wasn't the same then. He'd been a mere stripling of a lad, who still had to carry the goalnets and the string bags of footballs for his more senior team-mates – unlike in most other countries, where size of salary or length of contract indicate a player's standing within the team, German players know that they've made it when they no longer have to hump things about. (When Thomas Hässler, World Cup winner and one of the most popular Germans ever, was caught on camera carrying a crate of water bottles during his time as a substitute at Borussia Dortmund, the manager was almost arrested for vandalising a listed building.) Certain sections of the media tried to deflect attention towards André Trulsen, Stani's 36-year-old defensive partner, who had been at St Pauli longer than Stani himself, but the facts spoke for themselves. Trulsen was to be used as a stop-gap only, whereas Stani was declared team captain. At last, Stani The Man was a force to be reckoned with in the Bundesliga.

But it wasn't to be. Instead of coming out of the blocks spoiling for a fight, St Pauli started like a St Bernard with sunstroke, taking ten games to record their first win. Television frontmen such as Jörg Wontorra – a presenter whose oiliness must make his father-in-law hang his head in shame for giving away his daughter so freely – drew comparisons with the now-notorious Tasmania Berlin, who were enticed out of the regional league in 1965 only because the Bundesliga needed a Berlin team for political reasons and Hertha had been relegated for illegal payments to players. Tasmania went down nine months later with a mere eight points to their credit. Very nearly an anagram of Aunt Sally (had they realised, *Bild-Zeitung* would have added some exclamation marks and then had a few thousand T-shirts printed), Sankt Pauli were in danger of becoming doormats for the entire league.

But Stani refused to be cowed into submission. He faced the camera and stuck up for his team in the only way he knew how, proving the perfect antidote to the media-trained smoothies from the south and west. At one point, when he used the word *geil*, a yoof word meaning "very good", it seemed Stani was out to emulate his former team-mate Klaus Thomforde, possibly the only footballer to have mentioned orgasms on live television in a context that didn't involve scoring goals ("The privilege of being able to keep goal in the Bundesliga makes me want to come in my pants," he said, memorably). Despite maulings at home, despite chronically poor finishing, despite a spat in a mid-season training camp that led to everybody sending everybody else to Coventry, Stani remained true to the St Pauli maxim without reverting to the *Schweigepflicht* (the German equivalent of *omertà*) that governs most interviews involving footballers. He said it because he meant it: yes, we'll keep plugging away. Yes, it'll come right in the end. We're St Pauli, you see, we do things differently here.

What Stani didn't realise, or what he didn't want to realise, was that certain people at St Pauli weren't different to anybody else at all. They did things exactly the same as their Bundesliga rivals, only worse. Firstly, the idea of St Pauli being *volksnah* ("for the man on the street"), where punk rockers stand shoulder-to-shoulder with merchant bankers, was beginning to wear a little thin. It may have been true in 1988, when neither punk rockers nor merchant bankers ever went to football very much. But in the 21st century, a German international can go to the World Cup finals sporting the symbol of the postcard-punk movement, dyed in black, red and gold, without anybody batting an eyelid.

Furthermore, not all of the German *Volk*, or at least not all of the Hamburg-based part of it, wants the tatty charm offered by St Pauli. They want their football in a multiplex-cinema environment (some of them want their football in a multiplex cinema, full stop) with Caipirinha out of ice-cream dishes, not beer out of plastic cups. HSV, the big cheeses five miles up the road, in the multiplex-cinema stadium wedged between a motorway and an industrial waste plant, are *volksnah*, because they give the *Volk* what the *Volk* apparently want. That's why twice as many people go there.

Second, there was Stani's chairman, Reenald Koch. A former St Pauli player himself, he should have known what people like Stani were about. But his view of the rivalry between the two professional clubs in Hamburg teams must have filled Stani with disappointment. "St Pauli and HSV are just two brands of the same product being offered in the same market," he said. That's what Stani had become part of – the footballing equivalent of Pedigree Chum and Winalot.

Third, Stani was left in the lurch by his team-mates. As the second half of the season began, it was clear that St Pauli would be going down in the spring. Even the most addicted multi-millionaire gambler would have gone to the funfair next to the ground and blown his money on the cranes that grab fluffy toys rather than risk even 50 cents on St Pauli. And so the mass exodus began.

As Stani threw himself face-first in front of volleys, collected dead legs and studs in the goolies, and attempted to mop up the mistakes that everybody else seemed to be making, his colleagues were looking after No 1. Christian Rahn, for example, a hot-and-cold left winger with the gait of somebody who'd spent half his life as a pantomime horse, fancied switching brands and got himself a job up the road at the multiplex. Thomas Meggle, the midfield powerhouse who had already deserted St Pauli once after they went down in 1997, declared his intention of slinging his hook at the end of the season, despite pleas from supporters and team-mates alike. (The banner that read "Please stay, Thomas, you've got the cutest arse in the entire Bundesliga" should have persuaded him to sign a new contract, just so that he could find out who'd written it.)

Marcel Rath, a pugnacious-looking forward with the upper-body contours of a pocketful of loose change and the punching power of a finger puppet, blasted his colleagues on television for lack of effort, yet spent most of his time Fosbury-flopping in the penalty area and looking hurt. Jochen Kientz, a male model whose only claim to fame was being head-butted by Zinedine Zidane during a Champions League game two years before, put himself up for sale without telling anybody. Even Volker Ippig, the goalkeeping coach and custodian in 1988, the man who more than anyone else symbolised the leather-trousers-and-vertical-hair image that St Pauli supporters have been afforded, was accused of encouraging his protégés to leave St Pauli if they ever wanted to make anything of their careers.

Maybe Stani, in his role as captain, should have done more. A crate of beer after training, a cards-on-the-table session in the clubhouse, even a pig roast round his, with games involving tequila slammers, car keys and the word "romp"; everything or anything to recreate the spirit of 1988. However, although he'd managed to make people love him through sheer persistence, maybe he knew that it doesn't work the other way around: if you think St Pauli are crap because they play crap football – even if you're one of the people responsible for the crap football – then nobody, not even your doe-eyed lovestruck skipper, is going to change your mind.

And so it was that St Pauli slithered out of the Bundesliga with fewer points than any team had obtained since the introduction of three points for a win. Building work for the new ground has yet to start. After playing his last game for St Pauli, Christian Rahn made his debut for Germany. Thomas Meggle went to Hansa Rostock, but not without first summoning up a few tears to bite back and telling everybody: "What a fantastic feeling it is to play for St Pauli." (One can only hope that his girlfriend one day leaves him with the words: "You're a lovely, lovely bloke, but...") Marcel Rath has returned to his former club, Energie Cottbus, who play in front of fans just as hostile as St Pauli's, but for entirely different reasons. (One can only hope that he spends so long on the bench that he develops bedsores and has to quit playing and then has to explain to his children why.) And Volker Ippig's contract was terminated, and he is now said to be suing the club for reinstatement. (One can only hope that Volker Ippig disappears from the public eye completely, so that people don't have to constantly think of what it used to be like then and what it is like now.)

Holger Stanislawski played in every minute of every game last season. He has allegedly received an offer from Arminia Bielefeld, who took St Pauli's place in the Bundesliga, and are about as far removed from what St Pauli stand (or stood) for as Feargal Sharkey's solo career is from his time with The Undertones. Stani is approaching his mid-thirties. It's not clear what he's going to do.

Many people would say that Stani lacked ambition, pointing to the sloth fostered by being a big fish in a small pond. But Stani stayed at St Pauli because he knew his limits, he knew about arses and buckets, and he knew that Klaus Thomforde was basically right about what it meant to play in the Bundesliga. He'll make somebody a great predecessor.

royals flush

carolyne culver

It's a good time to be a Reading fan. They've won promotion, an ambitious stadium awaits First Division crowds and they've got rid of Uri Geller

Sunday May 27, 2001. I stood in Cardiff's Millennium Stadium, consumed by a growing sense of panic as an agonising cramp developed in my stomach, reducing me to a heap on the floor. So this was the end. Not only was I to suffer the spectacle of Reading throwing away their second play-off final in six years, I was to die a humiliating and public death in a concrete stairwell in Cardiff, my blue and white face paint smudged by bitter tears...

Was this God's way of punishing a born and bred Aldershot lass who had forsaken the Ryman Premier League perennials for the bright lights of Reading's Madejski Stadium? As it turned out, after Walsall equalised, and then went ahead during extra time, I'd stopped breathing and my vital organs thought I had perished.

When I managed to stand up and take my first faltering steps back out into a cruel and unforgiving world, a vision of hell greeted me: Cardiff's main street, still strewn with Saturday night's filth, was now full of celebrating Walsall fans. The queue for the park and ride resembled a line of condemned men, so we walked three miles in the pissing rain and I felt myself sympathising with Anne Robinson for the first time.

The eastbound M4 was a sea of blue and white clad misery as more than 35,000 Royals made their way home past Bristol and Swindon: towns we'd dared to hope we'd seen the back of. As darkness fell and the rain drove down, a Bentley cruised past with a Royals scarf carefully draped in the back window and the number plate JM 1. John Madejski was driving home alone. While fans contemplated the limp remains of £39 tickets, there went a man who'd paid millions for the privilege of watching his club miss out on promotion to the Premiership, plummet to the nether regions of the Second Division and then miss out on promotion to the First – all in the space of six years.

But that was last year. For once, "always next year" is a consolatory mantra we have been able to cast aside this summer – unless we want to start talking about another push for the Premiership. Twelve months on from failure at Cardiff, we could now dwell upon the image of a demented Andy Hughes carrying promotion-clincher Jamie Cureton aloft, and Madejski's Savile Row suit soaked through with Nationwide League champagne. The words "Viveash, Parkinson, Cureton... GOAL!!" reverberate in our ears.

In 2002-03, the Madejski Stadium will be hosting the higher division football it was designed for. The pitch will be graced by the likes of Leicester and Derby while our away fans won't have to fight to get tickets in cramped grounds. State-of-the-art indoor training facilities costing £1 million are being built for the Royals academy, and there are plans to add an extra tier to the stadium. Planning permission has also been granted to double the size of the ground's four-star hotel, all of which should mean more income for the club.

These factors, and the popular perception that we spent much more on our promotion-winning squad than any other Second Division club, no doubt fuel the special hatred Reading now attract from rivals. We're still in debt to the tune of £19 million, but most of this is "owed" to Madejski. He covers all losses, transfer activity and investments such as the stadium and the academy. In February, thanks to work-dodging Royals fans, the club secured a six-figure sum – part of which was used to acquire the services of Charlton's John Salako – as a result of the Football League internet deal that rewards clubs for the number of hits their websites receive.

Thankfully, because Reading didn't make it to the First Division last year, their losses from the ITV Digital fiasco were estimated at around £600,000 rather than five times that amount. But of course the TV money waiting for us in the First Division will be nothing like as much as it was supposed to be last year, and an end-of-season clearout was followed by little more than speculation about who might come in to strengthen the squad. As it is, we are set to lose £1 million in 2002-03, even before any new signings are taken into account.

Rival fans visiting the stadium have scoffed at the highly visible stamp Madejski has placed upon the ground. But he paid for it, so who cares if his name is plastered across the East Stand seating? Most fans would have their chairman's name tattooed across their arses if it meant securing the kind of backing we've been able to enjoy over the past decade. At least Madejski isn't the kind of guy who returns from his travels saying "Hey, I've just spotted this great Japanese goalkeeper and I want to buy him" or "I'm bored sitting in the directors' box. I think I'll go and ponce about near the goal and see if I can incite a riot".

Madejski's willingness to stick his hand in his pocket, while letting manager Alan Pardew make all the football-related decisions, has meant some bargain signings and shrewd investments. An outlay of £250,000 brought Jamie Cureton along the M4 from Bristol Rovers, while a tenth of that acquired the self-assured young left-back Nicky Shorey from Leyton Orient. Late last season Rotherham's loss was Reading's gain when we bought their captain Kevin Watson for £150,000 after a previous loan spell had proved he was just the kind of technical player we needed to complement midfield enforcer Phil Parkinson.

So, we're back where we were eight years ago: packing up and heading for the First Division. Despite our heartbreak in Cardiff the previous May, we managed to keep all our decent players for a second promotion push, apart from the former Tottenham man Darren Caskey. According to a *Times* article in March, sports scientist Niall Clark has succeeded in reducing the average body fat of our players from 15 to 10.2 per cent, an achievement surely helped by Caskey's departure to Notts County at the start of the season. The big-boned former Royals favourite left the Mad Stad in a petulant strop, claiming Reading had no ambition. The fact that he was left out of the line-up for the play-off final, despite being our third best goalscorer and master of the spot kick, probably didn't help. But his choice of Notts County, who struggled for much of the season, would be inexplicable if it weren't for the words "Eric Hall".

Yet promotion could so easily have slipped from our grasp again in 2001-02. We were without striker Martin Butler for most of the season and at one point only had one fit centre-half out of four. Goalkeeper Phil Whitehead – a stalwart of the first team since Pardew became manager – ripped his thigh muscle and was out for three months. Cureton missed pre-season through injury and he and strike partner Martin Butler (they scored 50 league goals between them the previous year) were distinctly lacklustre when they finally took to the turf together. And we almost sold centre-half John Mackie for a measly £10,000 early in the season, yet he turned out to be one of the most solid and reliable members of the squad.

Doubts also surfaced after an appalling run of form in late September and early October, in which we lost badly to Swindon and Brentford at home, and Stoke and Colchester away. But just as things started to pick up, assistant manager Martin Allen was told his services would no longer be required. Allen was popular with the fans for his no-nonsense style and obvious fondness for the club his father had once played for.

Supporters weren't convinced that the right man had been given his marching orders. But when Pardew took a firm grip on the reins and the former Reading and Newcastle player Kevin Dillon stepped into Allen's shoes, we went on a run of seven wins, two draws and only one defeat before Christmas, and the doubters were silenced. Well, most of them. Some fans will never be happy, especially among the misanthropic elements of our home support, for whom Pardew can do nothing right. Victor Meldrew might have died in the TV series, but he's alive and well and sharing the Reading stands with Waldorf and Statler from *The Muppet Show*.

No objective observer could claim they had much to complain about. No one did the double over us. Brighton fancied their chances after we suffered a gut-wrenching 3-1 defeat on a ploughed field surrounded by bus shelter seats somewhere on the south coast: our first away defeat in four months. But when the Seagulls visited us soon afterwards, and a top-of-the-table clash saw the media hordes descend on the Mad Stad, our top striker Nicky Forster was injured and Bobby Zamora showed little of his much-heralded predatory instinct. More than 22,000 watched an uninspiring 0-0.

Swindon, though, came close to robbing us of our dignity after defeating us 3-1 on our own turf in October. After we'd cursed our lack of TV exposure during the first half of the season, ITV Sport decided that our derby at Swindon on February 16 would be "an attractive fixture" (their words), and demanded, with only two weeks' notice, that it be brought forward to the evening of Valentine's Day. Reading fans reacted with disbelief and anger. The suits could have chosen from our meeting with Brighton at the Withdean, or a potential sell-out home game against contenders Stoke, but in their wisdom went for a game for which 3,000 away tickets had already been sold.

Maybe the cash-strapped company couldn't afford the wellies their cameramen would have needed to film at Withdean, or maybe it was some kind of bizarre M4 corridor birth control experiment: denying hundreds of Reading football widows and widowers their traditional evening of romance. As for an "attractive" fixture, it rapidly became clear that it would be anything but. The discussion page of the Royals' webzine *Hob Nob Anyone?* was soon brimming with indignant anti-corporate sentiment.

The prospect of an evening game on Valentine's Day, and the team having to play three matches in six days, prompted a wave of faxes and angry phone calls to ITV Digital. Plans to supplement the traditional anti-Swindon chants with anti-ITV slogans were followed by the suggestion that we should make it Spank the Monkey night. Alas, because none of us were hypocritical enough to own an ITV monkey, and a public and vocal celebration of masturbation was deemed inappropriate, the idea was shelved.

The corporate shysters even tried to blame the club for the switch. "The change was discussed with and approved by both clubs and the Football League," claimed a standard letter received by fans who lodged complaints with ITV Sport. It soon became boot bags at 20 paces, as the club told the company, in no uncertain terms, to desist from trying to offload the blame.

As for the game itself, Nicky Forster's early goal was ruled offside. Swindon's Bobby Howe tried to bury the diminutive Sammy Igoe's head in the pitch, and the latter was rewarded with a red card for retaliating. Swindon managed to get two of their own men sent off in the closing stages, one of whom had been brought on a substitute only five minutes earlier, and a steady stream of fans from both sides was led away to enjoy the hospitality of the Wiltshire constabulary. But, alas for Swindon, they still couldn't break us down, even though the ink was still wet on Stockport centre-half Leo Roget's loan papers, and Whitehead was drafted in at the last minute after three months out injured. It was so last-minute that he ended up playing in a Swindon top (we disinfected him afterwards) but for all the drama the game ended 0-0. "Attractive" indeed.

On the televised coverage you could distinctly hear charges of onanism being levelled at ITV Sport during the break – when the presenters were busy criticising Pardew's tactics, getting our players' names wrong and predicting victory for Swindon against ten-man Reading. Even the mild-mannered Pardew got sarky with the interviewer after the match and took the opportunity to have a go at limelight hogging referee Barry Knight, who forced so many stoppages that he spent more time on the TV than any of the players. We suspected trouble, because he had refereed the game at Loftus Road one sweaty afternoon the previous August, when James Harper's goal from a free-kick was ruled offside to the disbelief of players from both teams.

We began to wobble. Having spent 11 weeks in the top slot, our apparently well oiled machine spluttered and stalled on April Fool's Day, when Brighton overtook us and went on to nick the championship. Nine draws from the last ten games saw our ten-point lead steadily eroded and Brighton pull ahead with three games to go, with Brentford, Stoke and Cardiff snapping at our heels. Then we went down 2-0 at Tranmere, with only one point separating us from the play-offs and only two more games to go. But, true to form, two of Reading's most laid-back players – Anthony Rougier and John Salako – rose to the urgent occasion by finding the back of the net. A minor miracle, and a decisive one. All we had to do now was match Brentford's performances in the final two games and we would be home and dry.

The *Hob Nob* promotion party took place the following Saturday after the final home game of the season. If we'd beaten Peterborough and QPR had beaten Brentford the party would have lived up to its billing, but we drew again. The fact that we hadn't yet been promoted kept the players away, but Madejski did his man-of-the-people reputation no harm by turning up.

So it was down to the wire. We had to win or draw against Brentford at Griffin Park. Eleven weeks at the top meant nothing now, as promotion rested on the final 90 minutes of the season. As it turned out, the favourites to win the title left it until the last 13 minutes of the season to jump on board the automatic promotion express before the doors slammed shut. It was like Cardiff all over again: faced with a red army and knowing that whoever missed out would have their noses well and truly rubbed in it. I couldn't imagine celebrating in front of the Brentford faithful in their own ground, and they'd only lost once and drawn four times at home. But we had spent seven weeks perfecting the art of drawing.

Hundreds of blue and white balloons billowed out from the away terrace, while two young lads furiously rubbed the front page of the *Reading Evening Post*, featuring a picture of Uri Geller holding a football. They were either oblivious to the famous bender's previous ill-judged demands for free tickets and attempts to ingratiate himself with the club by claiming that he was responsible for promotion in 1994, or they didn't care and were happy to exploit any avenue which they thought might lead to promotion.

Incidentally, Uri still hasn't offered us an explanation for his absence over recent years. Could he really not afford his own season ticket? Or is his non-attendance linked to our plummet from second in the First Division to a fight against relegation from the Second? A publicity-seeking glory hunter? You decide.

Anyway, at Griffin Park, level at half time, we had only 45 minutes to hang in there. But then the inevitable – we conceded. The deafening noise from three sides of the ground drifted across our open terrace – a mere taster of what the end would be like. But the first person to realise that we would make it was the Brentford manager Steve Coppell. When the Bees scored he sat motionless and dejected while all around him leapt around like madmen. After the match he said he knew at that moment that they'd scored too soon and wouldn't be able to defend the lead, with Reading throwing everything forward. And throw we did. Bas Savage and Jamie Cureton came on to join Nicky Forster in a three-man front line.

Then Adi Viveash took a free-kick from the far end of the pitch. It sailed through the air towards Parky, who instinctively flicked a back header goalwards. Cureton simply lifted it above the goalkeeper's head and into the far corner of the net. *Et voilà!* We haven't stopped celebrating since. Those of a superstitious bent might like to ponder the fact that Royals fans were awarded the No 13 shirt at the beginning of the season, and Reading secured promotion in their 13th unbeaten game in a row, and with 13 minutes to go. Uri, eat your heart out.

While the rest of the country had the World Cup and the Jubilee to divert them in the summer, Reading combined football and royalty to celebrate the achievements of their own prince of the pitch. The skipper, Parkinson – half man, half scythe – has been a loyal servant of the club for ten seasons. Three years ago Madejski vowed there would be no more testimonials, because of the vast sums of money now enjoyed by footballers during their playing careers. But the fans were having none of it. To his credit, Madejski saw sense and gave his blessing to a testimonial match against an ex-England XI featuring Paul Gascoigne and Glenn Hoddle.

While the Royals squad enjoyed a holiday in Marbella courtesy of a generous fan, and the Biscuitmen and women of the *Hob Nob* site used promotion as an excuse for more bodily abuse in Reading curry houses and hostelries, Stoke unwisely saw off Cardiff in the play-off semi-final second leg at Ninian Park – never a good move unless you're wearing body armour. When we started to stumble in the run-in, we had feared a final against Cardiff in Cardiff: a match that would have made the previous year's play-off final seem like a holiday. But, thanks to Stoke, we won't have to cross the Severn Bridge at all next season. Unless it's for the First Division play-off final.

lost and found

david wangerin

The fight against relegation from the Scottish First Division occupies the next two chapters. For one jaded fan, brief hope and swift betrayal proved just the thing to rekindle his enthusiasm

In the end, they didn't go out with a bang. They went out with a pathetic little whimper. With a spineless, gutless, heartless and clueless performance that had finally cast them into the Second Division. It had been a terrible afternoon. Fans had left for home long before the outcome was certain. Even the noisy crew at the back of the stand fell silent just after half-time. So much for Trusted Football Cliche No 83, the one about teams never going down without a fight. A team had just gone down with all the fight of a garden slug.

And I had harboured such high hopes. Even when optimists were busily pronouncing them Doomed, I still expected fate to deliver one of those pleasant little footballing miracles we see from time to time. Away to Arbroath and down 2-1, they had somehow jabbed in an equaliser. Most of the travelling supporters were several miles down the A92 when this happened, but I had stayed behind and earned my reward. Miserably cold and uncomfortable, and exasperated by how poorly they had played, I nevertheless harboured a baseless suspicion that Raith Rovers were going to turn a corner. I hadn't left early. And when the goal went in, my suspicion changed to a belief. The season was far from over.

A fortnight earlier, they had lost a match which most insisted was their last chance. The 2-1 defeat – against the very beatable Falkirk – left Rovers in quite a hole, one which grew deeper the following week when they could only manage a draw at home to Inverness. At this point, only the mentally ill remained hopeful. But this team had played too well in too many matches not to start clawing their way off the bottom. They had a certain spirit about them, and maybe even a style. Teams with character could get out of jams like this. So when Nacho Novo bundled the ball over the line in the 90-somethingth minute on that blustery March afternoon in Angus, I was certain I had witnessed the catalyst, that it would now all fall into place. There were five matches to go, 15 points at stake and plenty of other crummy teams in the division.

I was behind them all the way.

The last time I had really cared about a football team was in 1993. Aston Villa were challenging Manchester United for the league title and I was regularly shelling out 11 and 12 quid for a spot in the Witton Lane Stand to help them on their way. "We won't bottle it," Ron Atkinson had assured the Villa faithful as the pressure mounted. But we did. We lost our last three, and United coasted to the championship. Distant second or not, it was still a vintage year, thrilling and rewarding in equal measure, the kind which made it easy to get behind your team. It was football worth turning up for week after week, the kind only Liverpool were said to be famous for producing. Well Liverpool had come to Villa Park and we'd played them off the pitch. We'd beaten United, too, and Arsenal, and even Liverpool again at Anfield. And on January 17 we put five goals past Middlesbrough to go top of the league.

Nine years later – almost to the day – I unwittingly started a relationship of sorts with another club. After the heady days of 1993, Aston Villa and I began to drift apart. Within a few years it reached a point where I did not know where we were in the league or who our next match was against. Eventually, Villa turned from We into They. On one of my last visits, I had parted with £23 for a seat in the new Doug Ellis Stand to watch Manchester United's reserves get drummed out of the Worthington Cup; a more sterile footballing experience than that I do not wish to imagine. It probably made the decision to leave the west midlands for more tranquil surroundings that much easier.

I arrived in Scotland with little idea of where to direct my loyalties. About all I knew for certain was that the Scottish Premier League was a ten-horse race in which eight of the horses were actually field mice, and that supporting an SPL team meant gathering up whatever crumbs of glory the Old Firm left you and gritting your teeth whenever they came to town. That seemed a horribly masochistic existence, and football-supporting was masochistic enough to begin with, thank you very much. The only other option was to support Rangers or Celtic, and frankly I'd rather pull off my ears with a pair of pliers.

So I developed a habit of attending Scottish League games without really caring who won. As long as the match was exciting and I had a reasonably good vantage point, I wasn't too bothered. Football was pretty much football. Kilmarnock or St Johnstone, Hibs or Hearts – what did it matter? None of them were going to be Aston Villa – and even Aston Villa were more a memory than a football team. The 2000 FA Cup final – Villa's first in 43 years – was disappointing not so much for the stupefying tedium of the match as for my own inability to become immersed in the occasion. The defeat by Chelsea didn't upset me nearly as much as the emotional investment I had been unable to make. If that kind of thing couldn't excite me, what hope was there for Dunfermline Athletic?

Modern football, it is true, had made me horribly bitter and cynical. In the aftermath of worrying developments such as the Premiership and Champions League, I spent a number of years trying to convince myself that Saturday afternoons were better spent in DIY centres and art galleries, and that the only football worth watching was played on a gridiron by the likes of the Green Bay Packers. There are still times when I think this is true, but it's no use pretending the game has lost all meaning just because television has grabbed it by the genitals – not when so much of your life has been given over to it and the game itself remains essentially the same.

The urge to go to a football match would still strike, and when it did I'd trawl the fixture lists in search of some sort of Match of the Day, one that did not involve the Old Firm whomping some makeweight upside the head, but was nevertheless significant in some way: a top-of-the-table clash, a local derby, an inter-divisional cup tie.

This took me on a fair number of uncommon expeditions: Brechin City, Cowdenbeath, East Stirlingshire and, on one occasion, East Fife, an experience I do not intend to repeat without hard drugs. It also did not require me to learn the names of players or managers, or to follow the progress of either team beyond the final whistle. I merely had to remember what the score was and make sure my nose wasn't buried in a cup of coffee when something exciting happened. I'm not sure this made me a football supporter. Often I would spend the journey home trying to determine whether I had actually enjoyed myself.

Better that someone asked me along to watch their team. Then I could have a go at making it my team as well. Even if the afternoon's play was no more exciting than folding bath towels, at least I could share in someone else's joy and misery. Still a fairly detached experience, admittedly, but one which sometimes left an impression which lasted until half past five.

There was nothing about a rainy January in Kirkcaldy to make me think Raith Rovers v Arbroath was anything other than the aforementioned sort of circumstance. I'd never seen Rovers and had no plans to do so regularly. They were bottom of the First Division. Crowds were thin and restless. Hope was rapidly vanishing. Stark's Park, a tidy enough ground, was a worryingly desolate place. For the visit of the Lichties, the Railway Stand was completely uninhabited and across the way maybe 50 visiting fans flecked the sizeable North Stand.

The match ended without a goal, Raith's first 0-0 of the season. And the rain never stopped falling. But it wasn't nearly as bad as it might sound. Rovers had shown plenty of industry and spirit, far more than one would expect of a team at the bottom of their division on such a filthy afternoon. I know it's not too cool to praise such facile qualities, especially not when British football currently percolates with the kind of one-touch players it has craved for decades. But in a team which had every right to hang its head and curse fate for not allowing the bouncing ball of the season to be kinder, my interest was pricked, and I don't think I can explain it beyond that.

I vowed to come back. I wanted to see whether this team really did have something going for it, whether last place was as false a position as I suspected, or whether I'd viewed a goalless draw with too much empathy for the Rovers fan who'd invited me. Instead of groundhopping to Who Caresland, maybe this was a cause worth following. I followed. When Partick Thistle came to play, fresh from their famous cup upset over Dundee and a 12-match unbeaten run in the league, I cleared my diary and took a seat in the South Stand, unaccompanied. And for the first time in heaven knows how long, I felt a slight twinge of nervous excitement at kick-off.

Within three minutes, Raith had bagged a goal and we suddenly had a ball game on our hands. The South Stand began to make some noise and the players seemed to respond. They scored again before half-time and proudly trotted into the dressing room 2-0 up.

The Jags, tired and uninterested, did not seem particularly alarmed; with such a huge lead at the top of the table, why would they have been? After the interval, they duly started to press. Rovers' defence began to list, but their confidence mysteriously held and they continued to create little chances of their own. With each Partick effort that hit the woodwork instead of the net, I could sense a home victory. And they got one. Last had beaten first, and beaten them reasonably well. It had been no fluke. And it had been exciting.

I tried to imagine the same thing happening one division up: St Johnstone beating Celtic by two goals to nil. That was preposterous, on two counts: one, St Johnstone would struggle to beat even themselves by two clear goals, and two, Celtic would struggle to lose to anyone, by any margin. The two teams could have met 600 times during the season and never have produced such an outcome.

One level down it was a different proposition altogether. The Scottish First Division hardly represents a blueprint for European football, but it's surely a damn sight better than the SPL – or, come to think of it, many of the major leagues across the continent. There is a real joy to the game when the playing field is not so tilted at one end and the media's attitude is so ambivalent. It's football for football's sake, a league you follow by showing up on Saturday, not by buying a satellite dish or reading your newspaper. I really liked that.

And I liked the Rovers, too. I liked their French goalkeeper, Samuel Monin, a guy who never seemed to smile or advance past trotting pace but still retained a peculiar charm. I liked his compatriot in midfield, Wilfred Nanou, industrious and intelligent and uncannily reminiscent of Villa's Andy Gray (the second one, the one who helped to get us out of the Second Division in 1988). And, like everybody else, I liked Nacho Novo, the import from the Spanish third division and principal goalscoring threat. The others were perhaps less conspicuous, but each was identifiable in his own right: the burly No 9, the wing-half with the bleach-blond hair, the full-back whose performances fluctuated as wildly as the Scottish weather.

However many shapes, sizes and nationalities they represented, a thread seemed to run through them all. They seemed as if they were genuinely pulling together to keep the club up. Whether this was fuelled by a generous incentive scheme, loyalty or an admirable level of professionalism, I couldn't say. But it seemed to show. And when Falkirk came to Kirkcaldy a week later and Rovers pumped five goals past them, it was obvious that these results were not down to any gulf in ability. They were down to enthusiasm, self-belief and work-rate. That could only ever take you so far in the SPL, but down here it seemed to count for a lot. And it had just taken Rovers off the bottom of the table for the first time in a long while.

Watching Raith knock the snot out of another relegation candidate confirmed all suspicions. These guys would be good enough to get the club out of jail. Falkirk, it is true, had been pitiful, but they'd been up against an in-form team. Four wins in six now for the Super Rovers – that was almost championship form. I began to sense what was going to happen here. It would be a close-run thing, a skin-of-the-teeth kind of ending which would probably hinge on that last match against Ross County. And they would get 4,000 at Stark's for that one and the place would be buzzing. Nacho would probably score one or two in the dying minutes while we pestered the fans with radios about the Falkirk and St Mirren scores. A real day of hope and anxiety – one with, I assumed, the desired ending.

It needed to be that way. Raith Rovers, one-time conquerors of Celtic in the League Cup and famous foe of Bayern Munich in the UEFA Cup, were staring at the pools coupon wilderness of the lower divisions, facing the prospect of a Fife derby not with Dunfermline but with Cowdenbeath. There were no guarantees of bouncing straight back up. And if that wasn't a cause worth turning up for, then football wasn't football any more, and I would take up gardening.

No no, Geordie Munro
No-no-no-no ma wee laddie
I don't want to go to I-da-ho
I'd rather stay here in Kirkcaldy

After the evisceration of Falkirk, Raith drew with Ayr United. Once again, I found myself passing through the South Stand, almost beginning to think I had done it for most of my life. Having played poorly enough to be thumped, Rovers were clever enough to avoid defeat. It's never good to drop two points at home, but just hanging on to the one was another encouraging sign. The run of one defeat in seven was better than anything they had mustered all season, and to have produced any sort of result after such a flaccid first half was yet more evidence of their character.

This, though, was a bottomless division. So few points separated promotion hopefuls from relegation fodder that drawing matches wasn't good enough. And so it proved. On the day Raith had twice come from behind to earn their point, Ross County and Falkirk had both won. Rovers were now back on the bottom.

They would stay there the rest of the way.

My late-season venture to Arbroath – an away match, for God's sake! – proved futile. So much for turning a corner, witnessing a catalyst. So much for a team being united by some special desire to keep the town happy. Everyone had been telling me Rovers were shite and I had been naive to ignore them. Where had I been when they were digging themselves into their early-season hole? And the 14-match run where they never scored more than once in a game – I hadn't seen any of that, had I? Didn't I know how awful this team really was? One more defeat – away to St Mirren – and that was that. Had Raith Rovers been a dog, the vet would have put them to sleep.

I turned up for the last rites, at home to Clyde, but I really wished I hadn't. The spirit and energy of the earlier games had completely evaporated. Rovers were now attempting to win without exerting any effort. The one element they needed most, the quality which had kept them from going down before now, had disappeared. Instead of being excited, or proud, or even just happy to have had a team to follow, I was upset. I had been betrayed by a bunch of tosspots who had spent the last few months raising false expectations.

Aston Villa spent the final third of their season in no-man's land, coasting towards the Intertoto zone they tend to call home. Three days after Rovers' capitulation at St Mirren, I happened to be in Birmingham and took in Villa's meaningless game with Newcastle. The tame draw was entirely predictable. There was every reason to feel ripped-off, cheated and alienated. Much against my usual prejudices, though, it felt rather different.

In spite of missing the first goal because of a late train, in spite of the £20 entrance fee and the irritating gamesmanship of Alan Shearer, and the bloke to my left who continually passed judgment on every Villa player on the pitch without once coming up for air, the giant video screens and *We Will Rock You* – in spite of all that, I was still terribly glad I'd come. I might have even loved it. Villa Park might look nothing like it did in 1993 and the squad may have changed two or three times since then, but there is still something for me to hold on to there, however hard I try to believe there isn't. And I suspect Raith Rovers deserve some of the credit for that, for helping me learn to attach msyelf to a particular team again.

I did not intend to trade in an Aston Villa for a Raith Rovers, and it is with some relief I declare to you that I haven't. It's probably not even possible anyway. This memorable season had illustrated the value of an emotional involvement, of not following football for the sake of seeing a see-saw match and a pretty goal or two, but getting behind a team and giving a damn about how they performed.

Maybe it wasn't Raith Rovers I had developed an affection for, but football supporting in a truer sense. My pulse may never again race the way it did when Villa were 2-1 up with seven minutes to play in the 1994 League Cup final, and my jaw probably won't ever drop as far as it did when Dean Saunders lobbed the Ipswich goalkeeper from the outside lane of the A38 to score the Goal of a Lifetime, but at least I can lean forward in my seat again and clap my hands until they hurt. However frustrating and desperate a season it might have been for Rovers and the Kirkcaldy faithful, I'm awfully glad it happened.

bairn necessities

paul hutton

Falkirk ended the season in the relegation zone, under a discredited manager and stuck with a dump of a ground. Fans thought things couldn't get any worse – for once, they were right

I can remember exactly the moment when I realised Falkirk were going to be relegated. It was about ten past nine on Tuesday, March 5, and Clyde had just scored their sixth goal. As these moments go, it hardly ranks up there with the death of Kennedy or Diana. For a start, any shock value was diminished by the fact that I was present at the scene. And since this was the 59th goal Falkirk had conceded in the league, it wasn't as though there had been any shortage of warning signs.

I can't even be entirely sure of the time. When the opposition score I have a nervous habit of checking my watch to see whether there's enough time to pull one back (or, alternatively, lose another one). But this was their sixth – what was the point? Still, if for some strange reason someone asks me when I first thought we'd drop, that would be my answer. Which I guess displays an astonishing lack of judgement on my part. Even by that stage we'd conceded at least four goals on five occasions. Quite why it took me 26 games to realise that we had a defence that couldn't keep pigs out of a close is anyone's guess. We were, after all, rubbish.

Still, it is quite surprising just how poor Falkirk were. Almost every supporter has had some cause in their time to start a sentence with the words: "There's no way we should lose six goals to a club like..." But with all due respect to any Clyde fans reading this, seriously, there's no way Falkirk should lose six goals to a team like Clyde. Especially not at home. I'm aware that writing this makes me sound like the most shallow of supporters, with an unsubstantiated, ingrained idea of some footballing order. And it's true, there's a chunk of my brain that has the idea that Falkirk don't lose six goals to "teams like Clyde" firmly etched into it.

But plainly they do. And that I watched this match without any great sense of despair or anger simply indicates how poor we were all year, and probably how stupid I was not to notice the fact. Part of me was in denial, and when reality trampled all over my baseless sense of order, it all seemed very, very obvious. To appreciate how I reached this state of detachment, though, you have to go back a couple of years.

The last time Falkirk made any impression on the wider nation's footballing consciousness was in 1997, when we made it to the Scottish Cup final, knocking out Celtic in a semi-final replay. That might have been our last result of note, but it's not to say we dropped completely off the radar. Ten months after the Cup final we were in provisional liquidation – a very rare instance of Falkirk being ahead of the trend in football.

As provisional liquidations go, it wasn't a bad one. We were out of it eight weeks later, with a new, fairly sensible board and a supporters' organisation – Back the Bairns – which had kept the club alive during those eight weeks and would carry on raising money for it. And, of course, our £1.5 million of debt had been consolidated into one big loan from a property company called Stadium City – though its involvement clearly came from a wish to be around when the planning applications started going in, rather than any feelings of benevolence.

However, that still left us in dear old Brockville, a stadium of the old school, without modern facilities such as seating or cover for most of the support. We've been trying to leave for years. I suppose I could wax lyrical about how it's a "proper" ground with a charm lacking in the all the soulless breeze-block pits other clubs play in. But I'd be kidding. It's a tip. A throwback.

Brockville went from irritant to albatross in 1999 when the Scottish Premier League refused us a place in the promotion play-offs for not having compliant facilities. Our board, rather imaginatively I thought, approached the SPL with a plan to rent Murrayfield – the national rugby stadium 30 miles away in Edinburgh – for a year. They had the agreement of the Scottish Rugby Union and the police, and had spoken to ScotRail about special travel from Falkirk to Edinburgh. The proposal barely made it on to the table, with every SPL club voting against it. Officially, the difficulty of segregating Murrayfield was the main reason. It holds 68,000 people, while the average crowd at an SPL game was, at that time, about 8,000. You could have segregated each one of them individually.

The real explanation was the feeling that Falkirk hadn't done anything about getting a compliant stadium in place. But with a town centre site that couldn't be redeveloped to accommodate a big enough stadium and which, for most of the Nineties, wasn't at all attractive for the kind of retail development that has funded so many other grounds, what were we meant to do? Toss a spectacularly unhelpful council into the mix, and you've got a club that's stuck.

By the start of 2001-02, though there had been some forward movement, we were still stuck. Changes in planning priorities meant the site could now be sold for a supermarket, but no one had expressed a definite interest and the council were still not on board. Faced with no prospect of promotion at the end of the season, the club made two decisions, each perfectly sensible in isolation, but bloody stupid when combined.

First, they decided to cut the playing budget by roughly 40 per cent. Despite attempts to stabilise the club's finances after coming out of liquidation, we'd continued to lose money at a fair old rate, and this seemed like the best way of stemming the flow. Second, they extended Alex Totten's contract as manager by a year. While the official line was that this offered the club some stability in difficult times, it was essentially a PR move.

Totten, in his second spell at the club, has cultivated a "Mr Falkirk" persona, never missing an opportunity to remind us how he never missed a game in the Cup run of 1957 and would be on the terraces watching if he wasn't the manager. This sort of stuff could bring tears to a glass eye (as my father would say) and is lapped up by many of the support. Amid all this sentimentality it's hard to remember that if he hadn't been sacked by Rangers, St Johnstone and Kilmarnock, he might never have ended up back at Brockville at all.

I'm being harsh – he gave us a trip to the Cup final. But he's a manager from another era, used to working with players he knows and used to having a budget that can be used to buy his way out of trouble. Most glaringly, he showed no wish to work with the sort of young squad that he would have to use in the coming season.

There were early signs that he might not be suited to this season's job. When it was clear the player budget would be significantly reduced, the board felt that players in the last year of their contracts had the right to know they weren't likely to be offered comparable terms. The manager said he'd rather not tell them – he didn't want to damage morale. Oddly enough, the news ended up in the press very quickly, along with comments from Totten suggesting that a wholesale slashing of the squad was inevitable. When players asked him about these comments, he quickly told six of them their contracts weren't being renewed – then included all six in the squad for a game at Ayr United. Hardly surprisingly, we lost 6-0.

Whatever Totten's failings as a man-manager or tactician (and I've been putting off talking about those) his working of the press is second to none. He's been around the game a bit, has a range of stories about his (brief) time at Liverpool under Bill Shankly and loves a round of golf. Journalists adore him. So when he trots out the line about having lost 17 or 18 players to budget cuts, it's slapped on to newsprint before anyone can point out that he brought in almost the same number. In Alex's managerial world, the answers to all your problems are an ever-expanding squad and a budget to match.

Totten's moaning about the inexperience of the squad and the loss of players from season to season became a constant theme of post-match interviews, and they grated. They might just have been bearable if he had shown some imagination in his signings or if he had a record of scouring the lower divisions to unearth some gem. Alex, though, knew what he liked, and he liked what he knew. Given the option, he would always sign someone who had worked with him before. There's nothing particularly wrong with that – anyone can understand why a successful manager might want to take a core of players with him to another job – but in the last couple of years he'd been taking it to extremes.

Alex's fascination with the squad he'd left behind in Kilmarnock reached frightening proportions. I worried he might be spending afternoons in his office staring longingly at a 1996 Panini album, gently thumbing the corners of the page. John Henry, Alex Burke, Mark Roberts and Paul Wright were all signed from Kilmarnock, and none of them could be described as a success. Some, or indeed all, of them could be described as a complete waste of wages.

Wright was one of the two experienced players Totten brought in over the summer. Although he has an admirable goalscoring record over a long career, he was plagued by injury by the time he joined us on a one-month deal. Little we saw in that time suggested he was likely to be much use, but Totten managed to persuade the local businessman paying his wages to stump up enough cash to extend the deal. Three months, two goals and innumerable sideways passes later (in one match I counted a solitary forward pass) he was gone. By then, he was playing so deep that there was just about no chance of him scoring.

The other experienced signing, Steve Watson, was even worse. The ex-Ranger (the more cynical among us have always felt Totten carried a torch for the Sons of William) had been playing in Hong Kong before joining us. Remember all those stories you've heard about the Far Eastern diet being balanced, nourishing, yet light and slimming? Don't believe a word. One of the slowest players I can remember seeing in 30 years watching Falkirk (and for any Nottingham Forest fans reading, that includes Brian Rice), he was only ever threatening at set pieces since on any other occasion he was still dragging his carcass into the rough vicinity of the action.

Maybe I'm being unfair. There was at least one occasion when Falkirk broke upfield only to bump into him heading back from the previous attack. In general, though, he spent his time ten metres either side of the halfway line, very close to, but never quite actually involved in, the action. It was clear to everyone that he was a player for whom hard work had made up for a lack of ability, and now, sadly, his brain was writing cheques his body couldn't cash.

With his touch in the transfer market gone, Totten set about managing his young squad as best he could. Which was not very well, really. Kevin Christie started the season as captain and a reputation as a reasonable centre-half with someone sensible alongside him to rein in his daft streak. A few weeks into the season he was being booked every game, often for dissent, and threatening to go off the rails completely. A thoroughly modern manager might have enlisted a sports psychologist. Totten stripped him of the captaincy and transfer-listed him. That the transfer list hadn't functioned in decades, or that telling a player he's up for sale now means nothing at all, mattered not a jot. A couple of weeks later, Christie's replacement was injured and he was reinstated. The bookings continued.

Lee Mair, on loan from Dundee – where his squad number had three digits – was regularly played at right-back despite a lack of any sign that he might be suited to the position. A spell in midfield proved no more successful, but when injury and suspension forced a switch to centre-half he looked confident, calm and poised against (of all teams) Dundee in the Cup. A week later he was back at right-half looking as clueless as ever. Eventually he tired of the regular dressing room dressings down and headed back to Dundee in the hope that 23 injuries might give him a shot at making the bench.

Such positional disorientation came easily to Totten. An accomplished right-back and a promising centre-half were swapped with comic results. A 5ft 3in winger played as a target man. Tactically, we were hopeless. One of a series of attempts to play three at the back saw the loss of three goals before we reverted to a flat four at half-time. Attacking or defending, if our original plan wasn't working, well hell, the management weren't going to change it. Imagine watching a team who, for every single kick-off this season (and for two or three before that), lined up entirely on one side of the pitch, rugby style, and humped it forward towards the wing, rugby style, in the hope of a favourable bounce. Welcome to watching Falkirk.

Maybe I'm being unfair. Maybe if he hadn't lost those players we wouldn't have watched such a bloody awful season. Maybe if the board had given him some more money early in the year he'd have invested it wisely rather than just signing the first ex-Killie player he bumped into in the street. Maybe if the two supporters' organisations that subsidised his spending had found a bit more. Maybe we were, as he suggested, just one more player away from being a good side. Maybe some of the youngsters just weren't good enough. Cobblers. We were rotten for one reason. Alex Totten, *j'accuse.*

The only ray of light at the club shone off the park. On the council, the ruling minority Labour group was removed by a coalition of every other political party and independents, and plans for a community stadium owned by the council and the club were firmed up.

The funding would come from a retail development (as ever) near the new ground, and the sale of Brockville. And since a supermarket chain was showing interest, that was looking more likely. After eight or nine years of trying, work might finally start on a new stadium. Just as we got relegated. Even I managed an ironic wee smile.

By the time of the cuffing from Clyde it was clear to even the most deluded that Falkirk were likely to be dropping below that dotted line. While Ross County, below us at the time, picked up points, Falkirk threw everyone a dummy by beating Raith Rovers in their next game, then going the rest of the season without a win.

As things began to look more and more desperate, a bewildering array of short-term signings appeared – to little effect. Former Ranger Neil Murray earned a contract to the end of the season after a promising game as a triallist and proceeded to get fatter with every passing week. Former captain David Moss returned from Dunfermline funded by fans' money, managed a good debut, was sent off for throwing a punch in his second match and broke a bone in his foot (surely the season's injury equivalent of the little black dress) eight minutes into his return.

We weren't relegated until our third last game – a goalless draw with a sheepish looking Ayr side that was doing its best to avoid any injuries that might spoil their golfing holiday. Faced with the reality of the drop the visiting support turned on each other, arguing over whether the manager or the board were to blame. It wasn't exactly edifying stuff. Supporters around me (young ones, mind) insisted this was the darkest day of their lives. We've all felt like that at some time or another, but it was hard not to feel bewildered. Even to a dullard who'd taken months to realise it might actually happen, relegation was hardly a shock by mid-April. With the enjoyment completely gone, I returned home and, like a chastened cabinet minister, resolved to spend more time with my family. I'd buy a season ticket, go to most of the home games, but give the aways a miss.

To many readers, that may further mark me out as a shallow case, too sensitive to watch my team in the lower, lower divisions. In a crude attempt at mitigation, all I can say is, I've done it before and I can live without watching a bad Falkirk side playing in grounds even worse than ours. Frankly, I just can't be arsed watching a tedious, boring team whose chances of improving under their current management are non-existent. And besides, nothing, but nothing, would make me want to travel to Stranraer ever again.

In fact not caring feels good – you should try it. Having a season so bad that I couldn't be bothered being upset when I got home has turned out great. I could watch us lose week after week, shrug the shoulders and head home to act like a human being. Memorably, I found myself described as "bearable to live with". The season even seemed like a bit of a release.

I suspected, deep down, that if I stuck to my "home games only" plan, I would never go back to watching every game. I might even stick to my promise of never taking my son to a Falkirk game until he specifically asked – I'm not taking the blame for all the bitterness in his thirties. I might even be the sort of father who takes his kids on trips that don't involve football. I may even develop a fully formed sense of perspective. Maybe some good was going to come out of the season after all.

That, at least, was how it seemed until the last game. Then, suddenly, the close season produced everything that the actual season hadn't. The club made Alex Totten director of golf (sorry, football). He'd refused to resign and the club couldn't afford to sack him, but he was prepared to move upstairs in a face and money-saving manoeuvre. Airdrie were placed in full liquidation and we picked up their manager, Ian McCall, their top scorer, Owen Coyle, and their vacant place in the First Division. And the club casually let slip that it expected Falkirk to be playing their final game at Brockville in December or January. Any depth I'd developed vanished as quickly as it had arrived.

dry run to the top

kevin fenton

Slovan Liberec won the title for the first time, a triumph for the provinces and for the revolutionary theory in Czech football that high alcohol consumption does not make you fit

To supreme indifference in the rest of Europe, a bitter fight over how football should be played has been going on in the Czech Republic. The two sides – let's call them the "old school" and the "modernisers" – have been slugging it out on the pitch, in press conferences and, most of all, on Czech television's *Champions League Studio* for the past five years.

What is "modern" football in the Czech Republic? It has four characteristics: the system (4-4-2), the style of play (hard working, closing down the man with the ball fast), training methods (lots of conditioning work) and lifestyle (no smoking and not much drinking). The leading modernisers are the former Sparta and Slavia coach Jaroslav Hrebik, Vlastimil Petrzela (who has recently left Bohemians) and Josef Csaplar (assistant coach at Liberec).

The old school is pretty much the opposite. The system is 3-5-2, with a sweeper who never comes forward and a midfield that is strictly divided between players characterised as offensive (can't defend, won't defend) and defensive (forbidden to attack). The style is encapsulated by an oft-used Czech sentence which means: "Our system is based on a secure defence." That is, we have ten men behind the ball at all times, especially away from home. Training mostly consists of 11-a-side practice matches and drinking is quietly tolerated, as the team getting plastered together on a regular basis helps to improve morale. The leading old school men are Frantisek Cipro (Teplice), Josef Chovanec (former national team and Sparta coach), Ivan Hasek (formerly Sparta, now at Strasbourg in France) and Petr Rada (formerly Teplice and Slavia, now at Pilsen).

There are also a few teams that play a sort of in-between style; sometimes they run about and sometimes they can't be bothered. And there are personalities that fall between the two camps, like the former Zizkov coach Zdenek Scasny, who produces hard-running teams but is happy to row with anybody. And then there is Milan Luhovy.

It was probably Luhovy who got the ball rolling on *Champions League Studio*. As in every other league, there is an unwritten rule in the Czech Republic that you shouldn't put the boot into a fellow pro – we're all in the same boat, etc. No player or coach commenting on a TV game ever says: "I don't think he's much good, and I've heard he's down the pub all the time." Luhovy, though, evidently couldn't give two hoots about that. He was a Czechoslovak international who moved to Sporting Gijón after Italia 90. He now divides his time between Prague and Spain and was frequently invited to be a TV pundit when a Spanish team was playing.

Luhovy made the whole Champions League extravaganza worth watching just for the 15 or 20 minutes during which he overpowered his helpless host. We cared not whether the football was any good, we wanted the "enemy of Czech football" to come on and tell it like it was. A typical Luhovy comment went something like this: "Barcelona rang me up and asked me what sort of style Sparta play.

I said they haven't got any particular style, they just sort of mill about." The joy I felt when he first put the boot into Sparta was incomparable. "Yes!" I cried. "Yes! That's right, they're crap. They're crap and he said it on national television."

There was one player in particular whom Luhovy singled out for criticism. A natural goalscorer who might have been good once, but who had declined sadly and now simply hung around in front of goal waiting for his team-mates to supply him with chances – Horst "Sigi" Siegl. The gist of what Luhovy said was that he was a fat, idle, overpaid (reputedly the highest earner in the Czech league) drunkard and that Sparta should get rid of him pronto. Siegl's reply was unprintable, but Luhovy repeated his criticism every time someone asked him, which was often, and in the end he was pretty much proved right.

The crunch came in the 1999 Champions League opener at home to Bordeaux. In the second half Vratislav Lokvenc took a dive in the box and the hitherto anonymous Siegl stepped up to take the penalty. After he fired hopelessly wide the stadium rose more or less as one and chanted *"Sigi ven!"* (Sigi off!) until Hasek substituted him. A man sitting two rows in front of me stood up, horrified, and tried to make the other 15,000 see reason: "Stop it! Stop it! He's done a lot for Sparta!" But that was Siegl's last game as a fixture in Sparta's starting line-up.

Getting rid of Siegl was obviously what Sparta needed and they improved enough to make the Champions League second stage that year. After losing 2-0 at home to Porto, they went to Barcelona, and from this game Jaroslav Hrebik emerged from Luhovy's shadow as a man equally capable of putting the boot into Sparta. By this time Hrebik had coached every second club in the First Division, but as he also part-owned a mechanical engineering company, he wasn't financially dependent on football.

His main pre-match comment was to point out that, as the referee was Pierluigi Collina of Italy, Sparta's midfield hardman Martin

Hasek (no relation to Ivan) had better watch his step. Hasek was sent off for his second bookable offence – taking an opponent's legs away from behind, under the referee's nose – after half an hour and Hrebik's grin at half-time could have been measured in metres. After the game Martin Hasek said he hadn't been told anything about Collina and Hrebik's star began to rise.

Both the media and the public loved the two of them and Luhovy, in particular, was everywhere. The establishment obviously didn't like what was happening and got even madder when he widened the scope of attack to include the heads of the CMFS, the Czech FA (strictly speaking the Bohemian-Moravian FA). He claimed that CMFS chairman Frantisek Chvalovsky was involved in some very dodgy deals. This was a little surprising at the time as Chvalovsky owned a number of respectable and profitable businesses such as pig farms and breweries. Nevertheless, he is now awaiting trial after being investigated for the biggest fraud in the country's history.

In 2001-02, Hrebik was given the chance to apply his modernising instincts to Sparta themselves, with revealing results. In fact, the season saw the modernisers make what seems to be a decisive breakthrough, although Hrebik himself was not the immediate beneficiary. The main battlegrounds for the acceptance of the new-fangled ideas were over the importance of conditioning work and Czech football's endemic drinking culture.

Players are gradually getting fitter, but from a very low base. The lifestyles of English footballers in the 1970s and 1980s may be held in low esteem, but they were model pros compared to their Czech counterparts. The three-day bender simply doesn't exist in England, whereas here they have been more or less obligatory after big wins until very recently. When Liberec knocked Celta Vigo out of the UEFA Cup in the autumn of 2001, the coaching staff took the players to an isolated mountain hotel to make sure they didn't get legless and could be found in the morning for training – a very sensible precaution.

This drinking culture gave birth to the concept of the "treasurer". Every Czech squad has one, usually a senior pro, and it is his job to collect "registration fees" from new signings and other payments from all players, for example for reaching a landmark for goalscoring or appearances. He then uses the money he collects to take the squad to the pub. Say a "registration fee" is 2,000 crowns (£36) and half a litre of beer costs 15 crowns (it can be half that), that makes a total of 133 beers. You can imagine the start of summer or winter training if a club has brought in four or five new players. When Siegl scored his 100th league goal, he voluntarily paid the club treasurer 100 bottles of champagne. Training the next day was not that strenuous.

The modernisers are dead set against all this boozing and have tried everything in their power to stamp it out. The most memorable incident came when Petrzela went mad at the Bohemians goalkeeper before a friendly at the end of the 2001 winter break – apparently he could smell the alcohol on the keeper's breath when he went into the dressing room – and stopped his basic wages for five months. That's months, not weeks.

This year all the shouting at players to stop smoking and run about more has borne fruit and the modernisers have delivered the results they always promised. All season the top four teams were the four that worked the hardest – Sparta, Liberec, Zizkov and Bohemians. The laziest team in the league, Teplice, are also one of the richest, being part of a multinational seeking world domination in the glass production industry, but spent most of the season battling against relegation.

The modernised sides have also begun to make an impact in Europe. Liberec reached the UEFA Cup quarter-finals and Sparta got to the second phase of the Champions League. The highlight of Sparta's campaign was a 4-0 home win over a static Feyernoord (subsequently UEFA Cup winners), when they gave the Dutchmen a lesson in what contemporary football is all about. Sparta also managed a draw in Munich and only lost to Bayern at home when the captain Jiri Novotny (once famously fined by Hrebik for eating a sausage at an inappropriate moment) added to his long list of howlers by sending a bullet header into the top corner of his own net.

The problem, for Hrebik in particular as it turned out, is the notorious impatience of the club owners. In the middle of March, Ceske Budejovice fired their coach Milan Boksa. They were top of the second division at the time, but the sports director justified it by saying he had "imagined a bigger lead". Boksa was also fired by Olomouc a couple of years ago when they were second in the first division and on course for a Champions League spot – apparently they weren't playing nice enough football.

It has been the pattern recently in Czech football for one provincial club to do reasonably well and get into Europe, but they don't usually take the championship from Sparta. That all changed in 2001-02 as Slovan Liberec consolidated their European success by taking the title. The club from the Sudetenland, near the German and Polish borders, needed a winning goal four minutes from the end of the last game by Slavia Prague's veteran Pavel Kuka against Zizkov. That handed the championship to Liberec, despite their surprise defeat at Bohemians, where they even contrived to miss a penalty. Nonetheless, it was a deserved triumph.

Last season was the third in charge for Liberec's coach Ladislav Skorpil, making him one of the longest serving in the first division. Whenever they ran into a sticky patch, which wasn't that often, the board backed Skorpil and everything came right in the end. Such stability, highly unusual in the Czech league, has been the key to their rise. They were also helped out by Sparta, who broke the golden rule of title-winning: never let your biggest rival have the best player in the league for free.

In the 2000-01 season Vaclav Kolousek was loaned to Sparta by Salernitana of Italy's Serie B, but in the summer Sparta's director-general Miroslav Pelta decided he wasn't good enough – he hadn't been a first-team regular – and kicked him out. Skorpil had worked with him previously at Dukla and brought him up north, where he joined centre half Petr Johana and Slavia reject Jiri Stajner to form the backbone of the side. Stajner had been thrown out of Slavia for excessive drinking, which is some achievement – it must have been measured in hectolitres.

Liberec got off to a great start and, inspired by Kolousek, won 2-1 at Sparta in their third match, but from there they went downhill. The solution was to hire Pribram's assistant coach Josef Csaplar, a younger man with huge knowledge of how the game is played in the rest of Europe. Csaplar changed Liberec's style to one where they started to put a lot more pressure on the ball and get forward more quickly. The change paid off and they started climbing the table.

Then came the UEFA Cup second round game against Celta, who were top of the table in Spain at the time. Slovan had been a little unlucky to go down 3-1 in Spain, but after the game Skorpil had said they only needed to win 2-0, a common result in football. Everybody thought he was joking until Jan Nezmar slotted in the second with his first touch after coming on as sub. Slovan played Vigo off the park in winning 3-0, and that gave them the confidence they needed to go on a run, cruising past Mallorca and Lyon (both 5-2 on aggregate) before running out of steam in the last eight against Borussia Dortmund.

Meanwhile, over at Sparta, Hrebik was having problems. He is a man renowned for his excellent theoretical knowledge of the game, but also for a complete inability to get on with players – not unconnected with his desire to make them run about in training and keep them out of the pub. After a shaky start, Sparta played some of their best football for years, but in the winter break they didn't so much push the self-destruct button as hammer at it repeatedly. First, they sold two first-teamers, Martin Hasek to Austria Vienna and Vladimir Labant to West Ham. As is always the case when Sparta sell a good player to a richer club (usually about three a season), each of the departures could be justified individually – Hasek is an ageing defensive midfielder who can't pass more than ten yards and Labant's contract would have been up in the summer – but taken together you have to wonder. In the end Sparta missed out on the Champions League quarter-finals to Panathiniakos by a point, having lost twice to the Greek club.

By the end of March Liberec and Zizkov had closed right up in the league and Sparta travelled to Jablonec for a game that had been the subject of much media speculation. The Czech league is perhaps not the most corrupt in Europe, but neither is it the cleanest and every year there is a lot of talk about match fixing. It was widely believed that the outcome of this game had been fixed and bookies were refusing all single bets because of the various personal connections between the clubs. In particular, Sparta's director-general, Pelta, had been president of Jablonec before moving to Prague. Jablonec, however, won 2-0, thanks to howlers by Sparta's internationals Zdenek Grygera and Jiri Novotny (again). That wasn't the worst of it though. On the way back to Prague the team coach was attacked by a group of Sparta's own hooligans, who forced it on to the hard shoulder, smashed the windows and threatened worse if the team didn't start winning.

Pelta did what he always does under pressure – broke into a sweat and panicked. So did the club's president, Vlastimil Kostal. On the Thursday after the game they finally gave in to the players' complaints about all that running they had to do in training and Hrebik was fired – they were then one point behind Liberec in second place. Hrebik's place was taken for the last six games by his No 2, Vitezslav Lavicka, another coach whose popularity with the players rested on his more tolerant attitude to alcohol and less than strenuous training sessions.

His first game, 24 hours after being given the hot seat, was the big Prague derby at home to Slavia. The home fans chanted "Kostal out!" incessantly, the man with the "Hrebik is God" sign waved it with increased vigour and the celebrations at the away end could not have been greater if Richard Dostalek's late equaliser had moved Slavia, not Liberec, a big step closer to the title.

After a 3-2 defeat at home against Teplice, the Sparta board held an emergency meeting and announced that they would spend at least £1 million in the summer to bring the next title back to Letna. That's roughly equivalent to Man Utd saying they will spend £10 million trying to recapture the Premiership – it's barely enough money to buy one of the best players in the league. To most people it was just more evidence of how laughably out-of-touch the Sparta management is.

Immediately after losing the cup final 2-1 to Slavia, Sparta appointed the highly regarded ex-everywhere coach Josef Jarabinsky. Last season he coached Banik Ostrava, who played fairly aggressive, dynamic football, and he won the league three times with Sparta at the start of the 1990s. However, he only ever stays anywhere for a year and his ageing legs may not be fast enough to get him to the bar of the Park Hotel faster than the players after training. Seeing as Liberec and Slavia are trying to keep their best players instead of letting agents tout them round Europe, Sparta may be looking at a second successive trophy-free season. The modernisation process is getting serious.

bitter orange

derek brookman

The Dutch FA compounded a miserable year for the national side by failing to appoint a Danish stripper as coach after Louis van Gaal's departure

I am told that the combination of altitude and prevailing weather conditions in Dalwhinnie, a town nestled in Scotland's Grampian mountains, means that grass there only has to be cut once a year. The growing season is effectively over before it even begins. Something similar happened to the Dutch national team last September. At a time of year when the whole season and all its booty should still be well within the (theoretical) reach of the more decent sides, a 1-0 defeat in Dublin condemned them to the international recycling bin. No World Cup to look forward to, no more competitive matches for a whole year.

First of all came the recriminations. *De Volkskrant*, a quality Dutch newspaper, hinted that trouser length may have been the root cause of the team's failure. Mick McCarthy, resplendent in his football shorts, looked like one of the boys and was clearly in tune with his players. The besuited Louis van Gaal, on the other hand, might easily have been mistaken for the team's accountant, and appeared aloof and preoccupied. Length of a different kind was blamed by Kevin Hofland and Mark van Bommel, who both said the grass at Lansdowne Road was too long. If only the match had been played in Dalwhinnie.

But the focus of attention soon shifted to the future of those involved. Someone had to carry the can. When it quickly became clear that none of the players were prepared to fall on their swords, Van Gaal's culpability and career path became the topics of the day. "I always see my contract out," he said a few days after Dublin, "unless I'm sacked." Sacked? Hardly likely. Van Gaal occupied so many different positions at the Dutch FA he would virtually have to give himself the boot. And he was still largely unrepentant – he didn't think he'd done much wrong.

Van Gaal had never made a secret of his ambition to become *bondscoach*. And when the opportunity arose, following Frank Rijkaard's post-Euro 2000 departure, he more or less spooned himself into the position. The new man at the helm wasted no time in announcing his target: to win the World Cup. He signed a contract until 2006, probably reasoning that this would allow him to win the trophy in 2002 then defend it successfully four years later in Germany, defeating the hosts 8-0 in the final. Instead, he oversaw the first Dutch failure to qualify for a major international tournament since 1986. Richard Dunne would be spending the summer in Japan, while Ruud van Nistelrooy would have to stay at home.

However, public opinion was still largely on Van Gaal's side – which made you think he would probably resign – while the man himself said he'd stay at least until his first "evaluation window" in May 2002, which tended to suggest he'd be off by Christmas. The neighbours, Belgium and Germany, were still in with a chance of qualification and could be seen gloating smugly over the fence. (Rudi Völler, in the aftermath of his side's 5-1 defeat by England, created a semblance of perspective by reminding journalists that his country could still finish second in the group, something that "the Dutch would be extremely happy with".)

The weeks ticked by and Louis remained vague about his intent. He would refuse to confirm or deny speculation on his future. He consulted several of his more trusted players, individually, to sound out their opinions. And, although he would not reveal what had been said during these pow-wows, the other participants often did. Frank de Boer gave an interview shortly afterwards in which he, as if predicting the likelihood of rain, said he thought there was a 60 per cent chance that Van Gaal would leave.

Most people tended to agree. It was becoming increasingly clear that the reason for Van Gaal's dithering was simply that he had never actually contemplated failing to qualify for the World Cup, and was having some difficulty in adjusting to the new reality. "Excellent at downgrading aspirations" was not a skill you were likely to find listed on his CV. It is interesting to note that, when talking about the challenges ahead, Van Gaal never once mentioned the 2004 European Championship – probably because Rinus Michels had already beaten him to that particular winner's rostrum in 1988. Louis had bigger fish to fry, although now it was more a case of the one that got away.

And so to Copenhagen, and what would have been a meaningless friendly against Denmark on November 10, had Van Gaal not decided that he would use the game to evaluate his team one last time, gauge their potential, and then make up his mind about his future. Despite fielding such intergalactic giants as Jaap Stam, Edgar Davids, Ruud van Nistelrooy, Patrick Kluivert and Jimmy Floyd Hasselbaink, the Dutch drew 1-1 and were terrible. That was that then. Three days later, Van Gaal told the Dutch FA that he would not see his contract out.

The news was not announced to the outside world for another two weeks, and what turned out to be a truly remarkable press conference followed a few days later. Van Gaal started off in a relatively composed manner, but became increasingly irate and unfathomable. He spoke of honour, about the orange tie he was wearing and how much it meant to him. He said he had been let down by the players' commitment and attitude. He would not, as Frank de Boer had evidently tentatively suggested, be more of an occupational therapist than a football coach.

In language eerily redolent of *1984*, he dished out marks for everyone. The Dutch FA: double plus. Supporters: plus. Players: minus. Media: double minus. Ah, the media. He always considered them more of a fifth column than a fourth estate. His offhand and belittling manner when giving interviews had become the stuff of legend, and in general was hugely enjoyable (far more interesting and revealing than the usual post-match drivel). But he always used to be in control. Today he was ranting, steadily reddening, eyes bulging. The conference, which in effect was a monologue, lasted about an hour, and by the time it was over no one was left in any doubt that the departing *bondscoach* was a very bitter man indeed.

But that was that. Or was it? Many people had not properly understood what he had meant when talking about the players' "commitment" and sense of "honour". A Danish newspaper filled in the gaps. The night before the international in Copenhagen, it reported, Kluivert, Frank de Boer and Davids were seen in the company of prostitutes and a famous Danish stripper, Kira Eggers, in a lavish suite in the team's hotel. One of the paper's journalists had actually managed to inspect a table in the room some days later and found multiple indentations in the surface, which, he concluded, must have been caused by a pair of high heels. Nevertheless, all the alleged participants flatly denied it ever happened.

But Frank van den Wall Bake, a close friend of Van Gaal, said the incident did take place and was the last straw: "Louis had had enough of this kind of unprofessional behaviour from spoiled footballers who abused their high-profile status. This is what drove him to quit."

Others claim Van Gaal left because his overpowering ambition could not be satisfied by a mere European Championship or a World Cup far in the future. I disagree with them all. I think that the real reason for his departure was that in Kira Eggers he saw everything that he lacked as a national coach (as well as a few things he lacked as a stripper) and realised the game was up. Think about it. In Copenhagen everyone knew what was at stake. Van Gaal had effectively issued a George W Bush-style "If you're not with me you're against me" ultimatum, and three of his most trusted lieutenants had responded by making a beeline for soap land. Kira Eggers obviously commanded the loyalty of key players in a way that he never could. What else had Van Gaal asked for? Commitment? Passion? Look who ended up getting it. There is a very deep barrel of murky innuendo that could be emptied to further prove her suitability, but there is no need to gild the lily, so to speak.

So Van Gaal was gone, and all the usual suspects were being sounded out for the job. As seems to be the case with international management these days, none of them was interested. The Dutch FA were keen to land Dick Advocaat, possibly because the European Championship qualifiers would soon be upon us, and few people can bollock match officials in as many languages as the "Little General". One can only assume that a special deal was struck with Advocaat to persuade him to accept, the deal being that he could use the position of national coach to further the international careers of all the Dutch players at Ibrox while, time permitting, also developing the national team as a whole. He was appointed together with Wim van Hanagem, so their combined height just about equalled that of Marco van Basten, another potential candidate.

Van Gaal lay low for a while, occasionally linking himself with some top club such as Manchester United ("Of course I would be interested"). But this was all mere smokescreenery, because seasoned Louis-watchers knew what was coming next. In fact, even single-cell amoebas could probably have worked it out given a few spare minutes. After achieving great success with his phenomenal young Ajax team in the Nineties, Van Gaal watched with growing dismay as one by one his brightest stars drifted away to shine elsewhere. How could he succeed without the De Boers, Kluivert, Overmars, Reiziger, Bogarde? The answer was that he couldn't, so he drifted off too, to Barcelona, where he was reunited with them all (plus a few new ones such as Cocu and Zenden). After a couple of years the time was obviously ripe for a new challenge, which is when he became national coach, calling on the services of... yes, quite. And therefore, after his departure from *Oranje*, it was merely a question of brushing up on his Catalan, waiting for the incumbent coach to get the white hanky treatment, then picking up the phone to arrange another reunion with some old friends.

As far as I am aware, despite her obvious credentials, no approach (at least with regards to succeeding Van Gaal) was ever made to Ms Eggers by the Dutch FA. Even other nations hard up for a manager also failed to spot her potential, because I see that in the month of June she will be appearing in *Bazar* magazine and *Men Only*, and not in *FourFourTwo* or even *When Saturday Comes*. Next year, maybe.

queen street blues

steve field

Steve Daley once cost Manchester City nearly £1.5 million. His recent non-League charges could only dream of such extravagance

I bumped into Steve Daley recently. He was coming out of a petrol station shop as I was going in. Nowadays he doesn't look much like a footballer who once cost a record British transfer fee; he resembles a company rep, which is exactly what he is. Daley grinned and said hello. He seemed tired, and I certainly was. We'd both had a long season.

Back in November, on the morning of the England v Sweden friendly, I phoned Daley at home. At the time he was coach of Bridgnorth Town in the Midland Football Alliance, and I wanted to check the kick-off time of their match. "Three," he confirmed. "Desborough Town, in the Vase. Do you know what league they're in?" I didn't, but it turned out to be the United Counties, and they had no answer to a slick Bridgnorth outfit who beat them 3-1. The action on the pitch attracted a smaller turnout than the meaningless international on the big screen in the fuggy gloom of the clubhouse. Daley stood next to us during the game. He was serving a touchline ban after falling out with a linesman in a cup tie at Sutton Coldfield Town, so he used half the Crown Meadow stand as a surrogate dugout, clip-clopping up and down in full kit and studs, shouting instructions while small children played tag around his legs.

Steve Daley is a forceful, likeable personality. Maybe he needs to be, because he's had to get used to being best known for another man's error of judgement. When Malcolm Allison paid Wolves £1,437,500 to take him to Manchester City in September 1979, it earned a talented attacking midfielder at the peak of his form a place in history as the biggest waste of money in an era littered with expensive flops. In his case, though, posterity is not necessarily a fair or reasonable judge. Allison's team "rebuilding" that year included the sales of City's established stars Asa Hartford, Mick Channon, Peter Barnes and Gary Owen, as well as the arrival of Daley and Allison's other signings, such as Steve McKenzie and Barry Silkman. Regardless of the quality of the newcomers, constant upheaval was the main characteristic of that period at Maine Road. Daley once reminded me of this, in a rare moment of self-justification, over a quiet pint in a south Staffordshire pub. He could also have pointed out what a good player he actually was.

Daley comes from Yorkshire and ended his top-level playing days in San Diego, but he has always regarded Wolverhampton as his home. He was at Molineux for eight years after arriving in 1971. He made almost 250 appearances, was ever-present in the Second Division promotion year of 1977 and played in a UEFA Cup semi-final at the age of 19. Wolves fans like him. Now in his late forties, he still has an insatiable appetite for the game, constantly seeking ever tougher challenges around the part-time circuit. It was no surprise, then, to visit Bilston Town, five weeks after the Bridgnorth match, and to see a familiar stocky figure in a blue top and white shorts barking out pre-match instructions to the Steelmen's Dr Martens League squad.

How Daley and his management partner Kenny Drakeford came to be at Queen Street was a story that had its roots in a torrid autumn for Bilston. During the 2000-01 season, chairman Roger Williams had invested a lot of money in ground improvements and players' wages, and had almost taken the club into the Dr Martens Premier Division. But then the criminal fraternity of the neighbourhood had begun to take an interest. Burglary followed burglary, through a brick wall on one occasion. Expensive alarms did no good, insurance premiums soared. Sections of the non-League press gleefully printed story after story on the so-called "crisis club", which served no purpose other than to scare off people who might otherwise have been tempted to take in a game there. The most recent offering had been a picture of Williams with a rottweiler called Bruno, with whom it was proposed to deter the culprits. There was no sign of the dog today. Possibly he'd been stolen as well.

After threatening once or twice to pull out completely, for which few people would have blamed him, Williams had settled for slashing the playing budget and announcing that he would sell to anyone who was interested. This was followed by the resignation of manager Joe Jackson, a former Bilston player who had been building a decent squad and a reputation as a good coach. He decamped across the west midlands to Stourbridge, taking most of his players with him. He was replaced by Daley and Drakeford, who in turn imported most of their former Bridgnorth team. As a former Steelman, who had ended his playing days with some distinction at Queen Street, Drakeford was a natural choice. Where all this left Bridgnorth's title challenge was another matter.

For my part, I was at Queen Street as part of a journey – a very complicated journey, which had already taken me to around 20 non-League grounds. Back in June, pining for a match to watch, it had seemed like a good idea to travel around the midlands, take in a game here, there and everywhere, and put it all in a book. I wanted to weave in the popular folklore of the region, to talk about its big clubs through their debt to the small, to discuss the personalities, the players and the politics. It would be history by stealth, traveller's tale and sentimental journey all in one. That was the dream. And the reality was a grey December 22, sub-zero temperatures, snow in the wind, and Bilston – depressed town, deprived corner of the Black Country, birthplace of Slade. Here it is, Merry Christmas.

The ground is in an ordinary part of a run-down area. The back of its tall stand gives straight on to the pavement, with the living-room windows of back-to-backs facing it across the road. It's flanked by boarded-up buildings, a Victorian school at one end and a derelict row of Fifties council houses at the other. All were barricaded with heavy metal cages. The terraced streets round about are colourless, with speed ramps at the junctions and kids playing around steel-shuttered corner shops. There is a contant roar of traffic from the nearby dual carriageway, and a gritty toughness in the air. It always felt like this at Bilston. The football club itself is a friendly place, but its setting is far from welcoming.

On the inside, the Steelmen's home had changed a lot in recent years. Once upon a time it had been a wreck, all tatty grass banking within corrugated iron fencing and cinder terraces held up by planks and wooden pegs. Now, the new by-pass had altered it beyond recognition. As compensation for cutting across one side of the ground, and to protect passing drivers from stray clearances, the council had refenced it along a touchline and behind one goal, using a space-age structure painted in Bilston's bright tangerine colours. Its value for keeping balls off the Black Country Route was questionable, and it meant fewer sunny spots to sit in during the summer, but it certainly looked good. It also restricted access for would-be thieves, and meant that people with expensive cars could park them safely inside. And, on cold days, sit in them and watch the game, celebrating goals by tooting their horns.

My odyssey had made me look out for such detail. I noted the new seated stand, with its orange and black seats under a flapping canvas roof. I recorded with a trainspotter's zeal the freshly concreted terraces, the hospitality rooms in elevated Portakabins, the hole in the clubhouse wall where the burglars went in. I clocked the man in the stetson who was always at Queen Street in some capacity or other (his job today was to make humorous remarks to people coming through the turnstiles). I realised that one of the most interesting toilet blocks in the Southern League had been closed down. (It was set in the outside wall and had one gate from the ground and one from the street. The outer one was locked when there was a game on, the inner when there wasn't. It was equally unsanitary from either direction.) And I observed that there was a good crowd in, that they were full of seasonal cheer, and that Noddy Holder and the boys had decided to give it a miss.

Bilston's tea-bar was in another Portakabin, with a hatch looking over a narrow walkway where the terraces narrowed towards the corner flag. In the midst of pouring curry over my chips the serving lady (who'd been there as long as the man in the stetson) was momentarily and almost fatally distracted by a near-miss for Cirencester Town, so that her patter ran: "Here you are, love... oh, no, he's dropped... it... oh, sorry. It wasn't new, was it?" It was only a temporary respite for the under-pressure visitors. On 25 minutes Bilston opened the scoring, and for the rest of the half their former Bridgnorth front line caused mayhem in the Cirencester defence. Both benches were going at it hammer and tongs; Daley was apparently between touchline bans, and Drakeford spent most of the time stalking his technical area like a caged panther. As the game wore on it grew very, very cold.

No description of a non-League club is complete without a trip to the bar, the main source of income for many and the social facility at the heart of community, team and committee affairs. Bilston's was very busy today. Rows of formica tables connected the counter at one end to the inevitable low stage and outsize Sky screen at the other. Windows of plain glass looked out on to the empty street, with posters stuck to them advertising parties, bingo and (hopefully) the West Midlands Police Crimestoppers campaign. At the bottom, a queue formed in the corridor leading to the scruffy toilets, where there was a constant buzz of conversation as old acquaintances were renewed. A gang of children who'd earlier been standing behind one goal came in singing the Wolves anthem *Hi Ho Silver Lining*. Outside, the floodlights flickered on.

We watched the second half from a cramped but relatively warm spot by the back wall of the club, surrounded by the flat-capped old men who were its regulars. As they swapped anecdotes about the Walsall Referees' Association, neon flickered along the new road carrying endless traffic from one end of the west midlands to the other. Over the shiny orange fence, through a gap between stand and school, was a modern art sculpture and the sooty buildings, chimneys and grey corrugated iron of the Bilston Stove & Steel Truck Company. This was a survivor from another age. At the same time as Malcolm Allison was destroying Steve Daley's credibility, Margaret Thatcher had done for Bilston's steelworks and the 10,000 men who relied on it for a living. The town has never been the same since.

The game had a dramatic finale, as Cirencester's Justin Miller scrambled both the ball and himself into the net with eight minutes to go. Bilston brought on their substitutes and inside a minute one of them, Martyn Naylor, regained the lead with a sliced effort most kindly described as a cross-cum-shot. Straight afterwards Miller headed another fine chance over the bar, and then the three-goals-in-four-minutes madness was completed with a heroic own-goal which guaranteed Bilston the points. Behind us, an off-duty group of home players gathered in the social club doorway, eating chips, drinking Coke and mulling over the latest scores from the Premiership. They passed comment on the subs ("Nervous – his confidence has gone"), the equaliser ("Oh, bollocks") and Naylor's goal ("fluke"). By the final whistle the ground was freezing underfoot.

Outside on Queen Street, orange streetlights shone on little groups of fans, finished with work for the year and hurrying home for Christmas.

And that's where the story should have ended. It was an average non-League afternoon, an occasionally exciting but essentially forgettable match and, for the Steelmen, another triumph in the face of adversity. My feeling was that the club were having their problems but would outlive them – crisis was nothing new as far as they were concerned, and somehow they'd always been there, playing at a decent level and doing their bit for a community without much else going for it. In a way they embodied the humorous resilience, the lack of pretension and the ordinary existence I was trying to portray. When the time came to give my book a name I opted for *Give my regards to Queen Street*. Bilston Town were only a small part of the wider picture, but they were a representative one.

Back to Steve Daley. By the time of our chance forecourt meeting, Steve was looking for another job and I was pondering the irony of my title. At the beginning of May, Bilston Town resigned from the Southern League after 20 years of membership, and soon afterwards Wolverhampton City Council took them to the High Court over a rates bill of £12,500. A winding-up order was scheduled for the end of July, so that by the start of the new season the whole dirty affair and quite possibly more than a century of history would be over and done with. When a senior football club can be put under threat for the price of a Ford Mondeo it's hard not to feel anger, sadness, even fatalism. But mostly you fear for the future of the game.

down and out

neil wills

A final season on England's muddy fields stirred memories of a career notable for exotic locations, sustained mediocrity and one proud statistic

It is a truth universally acknowledged that there is always next year. Well sometimes there isn't. At the start of the 2001-02 season, it finally dawned on me that my 36-year-old legs were down to their last nine months of useful activity and that, come the summer, my football boots would be receiving their P45 and a pair of golden laces. It was time to get out while the going was still good, or at least good-to-soft. And that certain something in the air, some barely perceptible sweetness in the newly mown grass, some stirring of my sixth sense assured me that come April I'd be going out on a high.

As it was, two events summed up my final season on the rain-lashed parks of England. The first was scoring my first ever headed goal. It came from a left-wing corner in a match which we lost 5-4. The keeper and defender conveniently collided with one another, the former looping the ball up for me to dispatch into an empty net from, ooh, a good three inches out. But, hey, that's the glamour and excitement of the cup for you. Everyone knows that in the First Division of the Ilford and District League, what really matters is getting up to the premiership and sniffing the heady scent of the Essex Senior League somewhere off in the distance. It turned out to be my only goal of the season, but that still beat my record for the previous three, so I was quietly chuffed.

The other incident, which occurred in January against a team called HB Wanderers (I never found out what the HB stood for – Headless Berserk perhaps), was an altogether different and rather more heart-stopping affair. Come with me to darkest Wanstead:

I find myself in possession around the halfway line. The opposition have retreated to some degree and I move cautiously forward in that way defenders do when caught in the unfamiliar surroundings of their opponents' half. With appeals for passes ringing in my ears, and still no one bothering to come up and challenge me (this being the second half, the opposition had had plenty of time to size me up and had evidently long since slotted me into the "people we don't really need to worry about" category), I do that thing no park footballer should ever do: I look up.

Looking back, I can't complain, I suppose. Twenty-two years I've played, man and boy. I've felt the studs of opponents raking down my shins in six different leagues, five in the south of England, one in Guatemala (the absurdly competitive Antigua Workers League). They have varied in standard, of course, ranging all the way from the not-particularly-impressive right up to the pleasingly mediocre.

It is a well known fact that amateur footballers have hearing as acute as a bat. This explains why they do not need to look up before passing. A mere clearing of the throat from a team-mate is enough to have the sonar pick out their exact position. This information is sent in a split-second to the brain which, in order for the signal not to be intercepted by enemy agents, scrambles it and sends it to the foot. The foot, with no unscram-

bling equipment at its disposal, blasts the ball randomly away. By the law of averages it must hit the target sometimes.

The one common thread running through every season is that, like Coventry City until recently, I have never been relegated. I once slipped a division due to massive close-season league restructuring but we'd just come comfortably lower mid-table so you can't really count that.

But on that fateful Saturday afternoon I look up. And what a sight meets my eyes! Who are these people anyway? Gesticulating wildly, grunting nonsensical monosyllables. And why must they shout – do I look deaf? I resolve there and then that it's the last time I ever make the mistake of looking up. Then, just as I am about to look down to check if the ball is anywhere near where I last saw it, a half-boy, half-whippet whom I recall had shared our changing room earlier, sets off down the right like a comet, albeit a sort of greeny-yellow one with a number on its back. Naturally enough, this turn of events gets me thinking.

Successes? Let's just say I've not had to build an extension to contain the trophy cabinet. In 22 seasons, I've only twice felt the sugary tang of promotion-celebrating Pomagne bubbles in my nostrils (Croham Road 1982-83, Kyriakos 1999-2000 for those taking notes). As for cups, I've lost one final (Moorlands College 1990-91 – last-minute goal, 3-2, the nightmares persist 11 years on) and won one (Kyriakos 1999-2000) though because we kept the same squad for the final that won the semi-final, a match I foolishly missed by being in Peru, I had to watch from the dugout like one of those injured players in suits the cameraman focuses on during the FA Cup final to attract our sympathy. A pity really, because our dramatic last-minute, extra-time winner might have helped expunge the memories of the 1991 final. As it is, winning it just makes me feel worse about the first one. Still, better a loser in a cup final than face the ignominy of relegation – a sure indicator of failure prolonged over an entire season.

"Let's just suppose," I wonder, "assuming the ball is still somewhere in the vicinity, let's just suppose that I clip it lightly but firmly with my right foot into the path of numbered-comet-whippet-boy. I wonder what would happen next?"

Sun, rain, wind, hail, sleet, snow, volcanic ash – I've sliced balls off my shins through them all. Played on all conceivable surfaces too. A few have been sublime, like Weaver's Field, Bethnal Green – sheltered, flat as a pancake, drains like a dream. Many have been ridiculous, though none quite as ridiculous as the public pitches behind the market in Antigua, Guatemala – if the avocado stones don't get you, the discarded animal limbs will. Once, taking a free-kick in a remote corner which boasted the rare luxury of grass, albeit a foot high, the ball rebounded back to me off a hidden breeze-block. Several surfaces, too, have been plain stupid, such as those early astroturf pitches – like playing on an ice rink painted green.

I raise my right foot and bring it down with a mighty whoosh upon the ball. The pass is on.

I made my debut at Duppas Hill, Croydon, as a speccy 15-year-old left-back and yes, I do remember my first touch of the ball in a proper game. We'd given away a throw down our left. The ball was lobbed up to an opponent's head but hit mine instead and went off for another throw. I was exultant. The ball hadn't knocked me out, I could still see more or less straight and I was convinced that that little passage of play must have resembled to the onlooker (had there been any) something not dissimilar to *The Big Match*, except that I didn't gob on the pitch afterwards. Had I known then that my career in the game would not see many greater highs than this, I might have got out there and then and saved myself a lot of heartache. Still, at least that heartache never included a relegation.

I think Kierkegaard had it about right when he said: "Life must be lived forwards but can only be understood backwards." For only in hindsight can we say if a pass was successful or not; if possession was maintained or discarded; which box the Opta statistician might tick.

I started off at left-back, not because I was a natural defender or, for that matter, left-footed (I'm not, as anyone who's rushed into the box expecting a cross from me from the left will testify) but because no one in their right mind wants to play left-back.

I gaze on as the ball climbs satisfyingly, now white against the muddy earth, now black against the ashen sky. High over the heads it rises – unaerodynamic yet airborne, spinning like a Russian figure skater on a gold medal-winning bonus of a luxury flat in the Moscow suburbs with central heating and its own entry phone and everything.

Injuries. Hamstring went once (1999-2000) – it's true what they say, it's like a guitar string snapping except that you're the guitar, and the string. Inflamed cartilage (right knee 1990-91, left knee 1991-92). Only major injury – broken big toe, right foot (five-a-side, which doesn't really count). Still, the most painful thing in football is going down and that's an anguish I have never had to endure.

Down and down the ball plunges, past the defender and on. Numbered-comet-whippet-boy, with the touching optimism of the very young, has continued his run up the right but is as surprised as anyone to find the ball suddenly at his feet.

What might I have done with all those Saturday afternoons had I not frittered them away playing football?

With one bound, he latches on to the ball. This is his chance. If only he can score now the other players will all have to take notice of him and stop treating him like a kid and calling him things like whippet-boy. First, though, there is the little matter of the defender, tracking back for all he is worth. Luckily, he is a dolt and a sluggard. Whippet-boy is inside him in a trice and bearing down on goal.

That's, what, 22 seasons – 20 afternoons a season if you count injuries, weddings, bar-mitzvahs and the like at, say, five hours an afternoon.

The keeper advances, laughing and goading the plucky youngster: "Look, it's that puny kid. He'll never get the ball to reach me let alone get it past me." Whippet-boy ignores him, coolly moving his weight on to his right foot.

That's 2,200 hours. Or 91 days. Or exactly three months, if those three months are April, May and June.

"The goalie's cut down the angle," the pint-sized forward thinks. "He may be an ugly brute but he knows his goalkeeping. There's just one thing he hasn't bargained for – a left-footed chip."

I could have learnt another language in that time.

Right foot firmly anchored in the treacherous mud, the comet whips his left foot under the ball and sees it loop high over the Wanderers' 'keeper as he strikes his fist into the air in triumph.

They say that even quite difficult languages like Hungarian can be mastered in three months if you work at it.

Uh oh. But has he hit it hard enough?

Really hard that is.

With the keeper stranded in no-man's land, the ball comes sailing down behind him. But rather than bouncing in, it seems to squelch in the mud. Painfully, it rolls towards the goal-line...

Or you're Hungarian.

...rolling, rolling, rolling, ever more slowly rolling...

Pah!

...a yard to go, a foot to go, inches.

Ez a villamos megy a városközpontba?

The ball comes to a halt...

Does this tram go to the city centre?

...but not before it has crossed a line and nestles in the long grass in the goal. Hurrah! Hurrah for Whippet Boy! Hurrah for me and my defence-splitting pass!

Some seconds after the ball has come to rest somewhere towards the back of the goal at the southern end of The New Wilderness Ground, Nutter Lane, Wanstead, E11, a defender wanders over and hoofs it away. The referee, not the fittest man ever to number a whistle, notebook and red and yellow cards among his possessions, sees this from a point quite comfortably inside our half and promptly pronounces that the ball has not crossed the line.

Needless to say, come the end of the season, my very last season, we go down on goal difference. By a single goal. Fab. Just fab.

contributors

Alex Anderson is a freelance writer and co-author of a book on Rangers' 1972 Cup-Winners Cup win. He spends a lot of time trying to explain how you can hate Celtic in a non-sectarian, non-violent way and support Scotland in a non attention-seeking, non-kilted way.

Dan Brennan has spent much of his life in various corners of the former Soviet Union. An Arsenal fan, he recently spent a season working with Tottenham as Sergei Rebrov's English teacher and interpreter – an experience he suspects has scarred him for life.

Derek Brookman is the poor man's Guus Hiddink. Both came to Eindhoven in the 1980s and saw success (Hiddink winning the European Cup, Brookman scoring on works team debut). Then came spells in Asia (Hiddink: Korean demi-god. Brookman: busker in Taipei). Both are now back in Eindhoven, but still have not met.

John Chapman is old enough to remember his dad taking him on the bus to see Duncan Edwards in the Manchester United youth team. Like most United fans, he lives in exile, and now works as a journalist in Brussels.

Unlike Sven-Goran Eriksson, *Carolyne Culver* has never struggled with the question of what to do on the left, having worked for Ken Livingstone and *Tribune*. She is less than impressed by her beloved Reading FC's nickname, the Royals.

Brian de Salvo was capped for England (in a TV commercial) while playing for Bromley Reserves. An erratic career in English non-League led to a brief comeback in Dublin with Drumcondra, who promptly went out of business. He is the only former League of Ireland goalkeeper to have directed a play at the Abbey Theatre.

Ian Farrell, 28, combines freelance journalism with a day job in market research, but divides most of his time between complaining about Manchester City, Barcelona and John Motson's unmerited exclamation marks.

Kevin Fenton was born in Stoke in 1971. Arriving in the Czech Republic in 1993, he decided to support Slavia, as they wore red and white stripes and their matches weren't obviously fixed. He learned Czech by reading the sports pages and now works as a translator.

Steve Field has been a contributor to *WSC* since 1998. He comes from Exeter, lives in Wolverhampton and writes on non-League football, principally for the Birmingham *Sunday Mercury*.

Paul Giess has just celebrated 25 years as a Walsall fan. He has lived in the north, south and midlands before returning to Walsall having developed more accents than an episode of *Auf Wiedersehen Pet*.

Paul Hutton has watched Falkirk for over 30 years – a process that has left him with a fairly jaded view of football, a deep-rooted sense of bitterness and a cupboard full of unsold fanzines. He lives and works in Edinburgh and occasionally co-edits *The Absolute Game*.

Matt Nation (Steve James) has lived in Hamburg for 12 years. He once saw Uwe Seeler in front of the city hall, but didn't go up and talk to him.

Exiled Lincoln City fan *Ian Plenderleith* has lived just outside Washington DC for three years. He writes regularly for *When Saturday Comes* and onetouchfootball.com, and is the author of a book of (mainly) football fiction, *For Whom The Ball Rolls.*

Neil Rose is a 32-year-old journalist whose first novel *Bagels for Breakfast* appeared in 2002. Circumstances sadly dicatated that his lead character was a Spurs fan, and he has yet to find a sufficiently outlandish plot that would draw Luton Town into the literary world.

David Stubbs is a *WSC* contributor and freelance music journalist. He has also written a biography of Charlie Nicholas. Based in south London, he lives in hope that Arsenal will one day soon do the sensible thing and relocate to their Woolwich roots – or even Blackheath, which would be still more convenient.

Mike Ticher is co-editor of *When Saturday Comes* and odd-job man on the *Guardian* sports desk. He has recently written the definitive history (in fact the only one) of Harringay greyhound stadium.

David Wangerin grew up in Wisconsin but migrated to Britain 15 years ago. He has contributed to *WSC* since 1988 and in 1993 published a book on German football. He is not married with two children, nor is he working on his first novel.

Neil Wills is a freelance writer and human rights researcher. He is spending his retirement from football doing all the things he always wanted to do but never had the time to because he was too busy being roasted by nippy wingers.